LOVE CALLS

Insights of a former Carmelite Nun

KIMBERLY BRAUN

M.A., CSP, MINISTER, REIKI MASTER

ISBN: 978-1-4834-2874-1 (sc)
ISBN: 978-1-4834-2875-8 (e)

Lulu Publishing Services rev. date: 04/01/2015

Lip to lip we suck the moment, tender, raw, free.
A word plunges me into you
A phrase opens the dark door of discovery and your Light shows up softly
striding forward to take me
My shoes and dress fall off as my lips reach yours
Without touching you I touch you, quivering
Without hearing your voice I vibrate in its sound
Without and within I go twisting and undulating
in the rhythm of your love....

This book is dedicated to you.

May life inspire you.

May this moment we have together breathe that inspiration into your soul. May you taste the elixir pooled in the center of your being. May you know you are loved, and are love, through the turnings of the page and the turnings of your path. May you shine with a confidence that has lost a sense of self reflection, and express to the world your individual beauty and wisdom.

You are needed and important in our world,

You are called to an extraordinary life.

Whether we ever meet eye to eye matters little,

we meet here heart to heart.

CONTENTS

INVITATION

You and I are about to take a journey. It will be one whose only limits are your own choices to open or stay reserved. Congruent with my nature I have chosen to write generously of my inner movements, states, queries, joys and sorrows, to relate to the world in all its groaning and all its exultation.

Though I traveled this way twice before, the first time having lived it, and the second as I wrote it, living memories are always fresh and new and this third time *you* write the history, the insight, the evolution by the way you open yourself in the process, bringing your own unique reflections and wisdom; and in some mysterious way I walk with you.

I invite you, in the quiet, secret place within, to let this book be a home. If my arms could stretch to hold you in all recollections that will come forward of the turns of your life, I would do it now, so hopefully here we will meet, you and me.

And we will find that we are one.

EVOLUTION

My understanding continues to shift and evolve. I wondered whether to attempt writing from my language then or write from my language now. Both have attractive elements. Since I am much different now than then I wondered if I was being faithful to Spirit present to return to something past. In the end I decided to dance between both languages naturally. If telling the story to cull the insight of the moment is served by using my language of the time this was my choice. In the end all that matters on the page is the essence of my relation to Love calling me forward. My own zealous devotion to the Carmelite path allowed me to find charm through language and to go beyond its parameters, recognizing its limitations. Perhaps you will not find this so, but hopefully you will let your own language draw the parallel and penetrate the messages that are contained herein from Spirit.

God is not a word I use much anymore satisfied as I am with the essence that is beyond words. And Catholicism, while an integral part of my spiritual formation, is not a community of belief that forms a home anymore. However two definitions will give you my present understanding. The first was shared by a priest who taught us a couple classes in North Dakota, it is attributed to a few, but in his talk he quoted a saint who said, 'God is one whose center is everywhere and whose circumference is nowhere.' And another definition comes from 'The Healing Power of the Human Voice,' by James D'Angelo who traces the word God back to Guth of Old High Norse, as meaning 'voice.' (Page 9.) These are comfortable definitions for me today.

I grew up with a personal God, one I spoke to all the time and I mean *all* the time. My childhood is deeply impressed by my personal God, and this introduction through my family is one of my greatest blessings, giving me the relatedness my feminine personality longed for in which to surrender.

So in my very being I am a bridge, of a living experience of a personal God to a living experience of Source. No contradictions, no loss of faith, only heartfelt connection that dissolves the boundaries our 'naming,' creates. Names fall short for they can never capture ineffable experience; however names are important in giving us one of the most powerful gateways to transformative surrender, that is, relationship.

VOICE

'It's all been said,' my inner voice reminds me, 'it's all been said. There is no need for your voice to express anything.' This is true and untrue; it is a paradox because creation has said it all in its very nature of existing so from that vantage point there is no need for anyone to say anything at all. Yet voice is one of the most powerful human instruments for inspiration, breathing Spirit that is alive and new at each moment, and so from that view nothing has been repeated.

In spiritual arenas there seem to be such hang-ups about putting ourselves forward as saying something meaningful. God knows I have had them (pun intended!). I chose to be hidden away where my voice to others was not heard and all my voice was turned only to God. Yet our voices let us ride the current of Spirit as it moves within; our voices let us connect deeply by resonant utterings; our voices create the vibrations of this Source by expressing its beauty in time and space, making up part of the very fabric of the uncreated.

Nonetheless, I have had to take courage in my hands to put this in writing. By doing this I stand up and say 'YES' to your expression, as for one, so for all. Sing your story upon the mountaintops, lament your losses in the valleys, rejoice and exult in your joys upon the countryside. Some of my most moving moments happened as my fingers tenderly held the pages of another's story and I have walked away inspired.

MEMOIR

You will not find a neat composed room in these pages, only sprawling creation rising and falling, building and deconstructing and building again until the message comes forward purified in the process.

When I was reading *Writing the Memoir* by Judith Barrington, she spoke of the difference between memoir and memoirs. This definition untied the wings held tightly to my side, constraining me from finishing, or even starting this first of three books. There she explains that memoirs are a chronological, historical recounting of events, whereas memoir is our personal reflection upon events in our lives. Undertaking the task of not only probing my life to cull spiritual fruit, but also of getting the 'details' right was more than I could handle. It also placed a burden upon me of how I presented all the players in this life of mine and the need to be certain of remembering dialogues and happenings with accuracy.

I have little interest in this level of detail or history. In fact, I think all history continues to shift even in the living memory of the universe as we ourselves 'move' forward in time.

The story for me is only the stage, the framework, a living myth, in which we learn and hopefully embody the deeper truths. This book is a memoir; all I share by way of story comes from my memory *now*. I had no journal, and even in the second and third books where you will dive into an immense building project and all its miracles, I had only my working blueprints, no records of names or timeline of construction.

My sole intention in all shared is the deeper message coming from within me. All the characters on the stage are simply players, doing their part that I might learn Eternal Compassion. I may not remember accurately but I will try to be as faithful to this level of reality as possible. Up front, my claim is to draw close to the core movements happening, the symbolic and spiritual story taking place which happens on levels under the storyline.

Disclaimer: All names have been changed except those of my family. My stories do not represent historical accuracy either. The events that frame my spiritual exploration may or may not be in proper order; I also give only my personal feelings and opinions. The story has been adjusted if my learning in the moment was through something that felt difficult or unpleasant for me, in order to protect and preserve the image and integrity of all people in my life, past, present and future.

What you will find here is an exploration of the deeper truth of finding Love arising within me. The story line is in service to this theme. Every person has been an exquisite teacher and for them all I am grateful. I generously share my feelings and my perceptions, which are only my lens through which any circumstance is viewed; the story is subjective.

There is within me light and dark in a dance of expression and growth, the direct object of my three books. These concepts give me language around the movement of Spirit. There is light and dark source within every element of creation including the human structures we create and choose. This is not a story for those wanting judgments. I am a lover seeking my Beloved. This is my motive and I invite you to hold the same motive as me as you read. If you do, you will touch the Divine within yourself. The 'truth,' if you want to name it so, is what is revealed and discovered within, and in this solitary place, Love calls.

LESSON OF SPIRIT

The date was August 6th, 1990, the Feast of the Transfiguration. Up to about a week before this date my Carmelite calling rang strong in my heart moving like a storming force from the love affair raging in my soul. What a gift to be given such clear direction for my life, and the song within sang with enduring sweetness. My love and my longing were all caught up in the one thing necessary and the one thing that captivated my attention, that is, union with God as a Carmelite monastic nun.

From the moment I read Teresa of Avila's autobiography as a twenty year old, and not long after the *Story of a Soul*, the life of Therese of Lisieux, the Carmelite mystics showed themselves as dear friends. They were the ones where I felt 'understood,' and at home to be myself.

We will return to all these Carmelite friends. For now, as a perfect introduction, this date opens the door between us. The four years leading up to this moment there was a certain pursuing of God that fired my soul towards monastic life, and any consideration to the contrary led to discomfort on varying levels, and choices that led to dead ends, until I returned to this path. Spirit guided me very, very, clearly.

Carmel was in all my dreams. After receiving the books mentioned above, recognizing within myself the same life purpose, I used to hike at Point Lobos near Carmel and stand breathless with the monastery Carmel by the Sea in the distance dreaming of spending my days and my nights forever within its walls.

But this monastery was full, with a waiting list that might keep me hoping for two to three years.

So I decided to get on with an undergraduate degree while looking for 'my' monastery. Sinking into the intensely charismatic University of Steubenville concentrating on Theology and Nursing, was the ideal matrix to nurture the natural contemplative path within. This university was unique, caught up in what was called life in the Spirit where gifts of healing and prophecy abounded, and most all found their identities from a place of prayer and healing versus academic achievement.

My lesson of Spirit, the focus of this introduction, came after a full YES to a call to be Carmelite. By this time I had visited a Carmelite community in Pennsylvania numerous times. Endeared by the architecture replicating one of my best friends, Therese of Lisieux A French Carmelite from the late 1800s, I was set to enter as a postulant. A postulant is name given to a woman trying out the life for a short period of time. Even the speak room meeting went famously as the prioress (leader of the community) not only held the customary meeting with me, but brought in the entire community on our second visit in just one day, such was her confidence.

This second larger meeting my mom, dad and little brother were with me as well. Holding Adam cheek to cheek we looked into the grille and the prioress said fateful words about my appearance, 'You have a universal vocation.' While it was in response to the nuns commenting on how I looked like a family relative or friend, the comment would follow me all my life. Knowing it has to be a soul resonance everywhere I go people tell me I remind them of someone close. Fortunately it is always someone with whom they felt a love and connection.

My parents are amazing individuals, now married to other partners, equally amazing; my parents were people who truly supported their children's dreams. They stood and stand behind us not only with words of encouragement, but with their actions. After a jolting lunch where I told them my decision to leave school and enter the monastery, they rallied their spirits to drive me to visit the very place I hoped to spend the rest of my life. They knew of my natural abilities and love of school and must have restrained their disappointment in my abandoning the notion of a degree.

Degrees always seemed kind of arbitrary to me if they didn't serve a direct passion. It never made sense to get a degree without any motive other than the accomplishment. While I understand the doors that can be opened by having the credential, I also have found that when one is connected with their passion all things fall into place and the degree, if needed, is a part of the equation. Since what I felt was my calling had nothing to do with a formal degree (aside from entering the mystic school of Christ as my Carmelite Constitutions put so well,) leaving school did not create disappointment in my heart. But that is just me. My parents had worked so hard for us children to have options and my choice had to have been hard, especially for my mom who was not supported in her own brilliance to develop her intelligence with higher degrees through university, and hoped for such opportunities for me.

With the initial meetings over and plans for entering as a trial candidate on the books, I was sailing high, so high, my whole body felt like I had wings, 'Finally,' was the buzz word. 'Finally...Finally...Finally I will be with you my Love, my Lord, Finally.'

The plan was for me to join the Carmelites for my trial venture on the

Feast of the Assumption of Mary on August 15th. I had asked for this day, it was the same day I had joined the Maximilian Kolbe movement in Santa Cruz, California called the Knights of the Immaculata and Mary (the Mother of God in Christianity) was my best friend. Imagine the excitement to hear them say 'yes!' All was now in order in my world.

I withdrew from university life, and prepared my things. Knowing I would have the chance to leave to tie up ends there was little attention given to my few possessions Meditation and contemplation consumed my days as I stayed the summer as helping staff for the University of Steubenville's' rich charismatic retreats cascading upon the campus in waves week after week.

Another friend of mine, Michelle, joined me in cleaning rooms and preparing for transition days. It was a carefree time and while we could not attend the retreats, we could attend the liturgies. The real juice was in the Liturgies anyway, they would last for hours with crazy songs invoking spontaneous dance, speaking in tongues and dramatic healings throughout. In the evenings we would meander our way to the Portiuncula where Exposition would take place until midnight. Heaven on earth was my daily lot.

One of the first few days of August I called to speak with the prioress, to find out what I should plan to bring and when I should arrive. Being put on hold for a very long time, my waiting felt like half hour or more. Even though the feelings of worry began to escalate, I remembered that she might be clear on the other side of the complex, or maybe caught in an important moment with another sister. I undertook the practice of trust until she answered and her tone sent chills through me. "I was gardening, Kimberly." Leading to what felt like a long pause, "We think you should finish your degree first. You are so young."

My soul plummeted. I was dumbfounded and anguished inside. 'We were so close to the entrance date, why hadn't they called me? Why was I allowed to prepare to join them without knowing the change in their decision? But,' I softly asked, 'we had such a great meeting and I have been preparing for months', my voice trailed off.

My hand placed the receiver back into its cradle while confusion muddied the former peace of my soul. It wasn't so much about her, but in relation to God. It felt like my trust in acting was all wrong. Had I been duped? Had I made it all up? All the nights and days lost in contemplation and union, all the inspiration coming from the Carmelites that were now my friends, all the sense of purpose and meaning and the motivation it gave to my sense of life purpose. 'What was all of that?' Thoughts whirled about like a stormy sea.

After the call, I ran out to the back of the campus where large open land met trees. It was a place I used to dance under the moon in love with my Beloved, and there I wept in God's arms. My weeping was so great I let myself fall upon the ground and sobs copiously flowed upon the ground that held me.

Even with the support of close friends just as confused as I, the days were sad. I entered a time of sad waiting, having prepared everything to join them. What else could I do? 'Should I look into other communities?' When I thought about it, I had no idea what to do next. So I waited and let go, sitting silent like Job did in the Hebrew texts so the waters would not be muddied by ideas on things.

Rotely my feet carried my body to Liturgy, my hands changed sheets for retreatants and my life continued its progression in time for days that felt like years. The Feast of the Transfiguration, August 6th, found me sitting in a solitary pew at the quiet spoken 8:30am liturgy. Five minutes into the service, a fellow student proclaimed the first reading from the podium. The story was familiar, yet the words seemed to alight upon my heart, bringing with them a sweet renewing.

It is a familiar human experience, to hear something we have heard many times in a completely new way.

Grace revealed a message. The story was of the Hebrew prophet Elijah towards the end of a tumultuous prophetic path yielding what seemed like small results. Elijah had just produced fire from a prayer that set on fire a dry gathering of wood, and won a contest against 100 prophets of Queen Jezebel. It was a victory ordained by God (in whose presence Elijah stood, as the text says repeatedly like a tag line,) and the hoped outcome would be that the people of Israel would return to following the monotheistic God.

The miracle did not work. Even worse, it set Jezebel into a fury toward Elijah with threats to kill him. So he fled to the desert where alone and disillusioned, he vented his anger against God. Even in his anger, God would send ravens to feed him and grow trees to give him shade. At some point, Elijah received a message to go to a cave of Carmel (a reassuring message for me) where he was to await a visit from the Lord. Sad, angry, and disheartened Elijah huddled in the cave without any guidance on how to hear God or what sign or presence God would take. Unknown to himself, Elijah's soul was so pure he could hear God. First, an earthquake went by, but God was not in the earthquake; then a fire went by, but God was not in the fire; then a raging storm went by but God was not in the storm either. After all of these loud happenings the smallest of breezes passed.

When Elijah heard the breeze, he went to the mouth of the cave and covered his face for he knew Lord was passing.

The words gently wrapped their fingers around my heart and brought me to inner absorption. I was there at that very mouth of the cave with God alone and in the smallest whisper, the silence sounded. Carmel was my calling.

Peace ensued with an unshakeable certainty.

The rejection of the prioress and the Carmelite community was the way God used to simplify me and increase my inner freedom. Gone were all the doubtful musings wondering 'if" I was meant to be Carmelite. Only one question remained: 'where' am I meant to be Carmelite?

The fun then began as my spiritual director, Father Bernard (now deceased) and I began investigating possible monasteries. The adventure became a playground of waiting to receive responses, learning about their different lifestyles, and being affirmed in their eagerness to speak with me. Terre Haute was high on my list, while Erie, Pennsylvania and Louisville, Kentucky were strong possibilities as well. Father Bernard always had time everyone. The specialness of our friendship was felt by hundreds of other students. It was baffling to consider how he had so much time and be so available, treating people like he had all the time in the world. I leaned into his care and our common love of Mary was a source of continual sharing as we speckled it with monastery brochures.

Only weeks after August 6th, the summer retreats gave way to a new school year. I was unable to attend that year, so wistfully Michelle and I spent every waking moment finishing our last tasks. Couched in ritual, the university prepared for its crowning end of summer Liturgy situated in a large, white tent outside to accommodate larger numbers of people. So many showed up to worship that the tent served as a small offering cover for about a thousand of us, while the rest of the assembly tumbled in every direction upon the grass.

Large liturgies like this always started with this alluring, mystical air as the musicians would tune their instruments. Guitars, flutes, drums, and voices created a cacophony of excited expectation. The pervading chaos would usually pull me into sweet silence and today was no different. Knowing it was my last Mass increased the level of intensity. I wanted to be there, fully there and not miss one drop of the dripping Spirit. The president of the university, Father Matthew, presided with eight or so other priests, including the beloved Father Bernard.

The charismatic priest stood at the microphone weaving inspired words through his homily, provoking tears of acknowledgment from each of us as One Body of Christ. Then he paused, looking intently at all of us. 'God,' he said with conviction, 'never withdraws his call or his grace.' The trickle of tears already running down my face turned into a stream. Spirit was speaking and the word was not lost, 'I love you my God, I love you! I will find the Carmelite community you have destined for me.' The wordless promise met Father Matthew's unassuming proclamation.

The last song followed. A "last" song here is a pretty loose term. It could have gone on for half an hour, or even led into other songs depending on the movement of the assembly.

A solitary chord on a guitar was strummed, and multiple voices intoned upon its fading, 'It is gooooood, to pra-a-aise the Lord....'not missing a beat, we all joined in with one voice, 'a-a-a-a-and make musi-i-i-ic to your na-a-ame oh Go-o-od most H-i-iigh...'

'To proclaim your love and faith-ful-ness, all the day and all the ni-i-i-ight...' All the instruments swelled into playing, as bodies moved into aisles to begin their sway. Michelle and I stood close, raising our hands high in a sweet sisterly dance, sometimes interlacing fingers. And we danced, all of us, we danced and sang with abandon, moving like joyful waves of water.

Father Bernard and I had one final meeting, where he placed within my hand a fateful brochure, 'I was just walking across campus,' he said non-chalantly, 'and another priest placed this in my hands. Maybe you want it?' His eyes had a glint of knowing.

There, my mission began.

SECTION ONE
Formative Recollections

Our feet will never pass this way again...my love
Your scent,
  it intoxicates, flares the nostrils and the canals within
pulls and pushes my surrender through marshes and explosive skies
where shafts of unencumbered light lay the land low
Breadth dissolving height and depth
Breathed....Breathed again....Breathed again...
Our hearts, never will they pass
  this way
    again

How MANY TIMES HAVE people asked me over the past 12 years, 'Why did you enter a monastery?' And even more often I have been asked, 'Why did you leave?' At first I did not know how to answer the second question, how do I tell a stranger about something as intimate as my leaving a lifestyle that was my entire world and ended like a divorce? The question felt insensitive to the magnitude of the choice. Soon after, I realized that most people look at it like it was a career change and had no idea the level of personal change involved in such a decision that goes from little things like wearing normal clothes again after 11 years of a religious habit, to the all consuming choice to ask for my vows (taken for life) to be dissolved. So I had to really think, 'what do I say?' What can

I say that is true, yet honors my own privacy? There was really only one answer, sometimes dissatisfying to the one asking, but at least captured the answer in a nutshell. 'I left and I entered for the same reason, to be true to my own personal journey. I entered for the sake of Love and I left for the same reason,' are my honest words. Void of juicy details, yet honestly true, it always vets the discussion that follows. Those interested in that level seem to jettison into sharing similar desires. But my life has always had this simple rudder. Even amidst my own complications and bumbling choices, and at times, downright unhealthy paths, it has not been long before this simple awareness would come to either haunt me in my dark moment or rouse me into deeper love of God and I would return to the pivotal event of my childhood. Any story always begins at the beginning, and so we begin the Carmelite journey in Cincinnati, Ohio.

CHAPTER ONE

Smallwood Lane

It is when we sit listening
Allowing the echoes of the world to resound within
Far away from the incessant, repetitious musing of our minds
We begin to hear the melody of a song that sounds familiar

Chords magnify, harmony multiplies
A chorus reveals itself

The very song of our lineage comes back to us.
A-a-ah yes, it is a song you used to sing many lives ago
A song of love and life

A song we have yet to finish
Really we have only begun
And as we melt into the symphony
A sense of sweet joy returns
We re-member the reasons for which we have come

I WAS EITHER 5 or 6 years old as I remember. We lived at 8474 Smallwood Lane at the end of a cul-de-sac in a small section called Blue Ash, a suburb of Cincinnati, Ohio. Because the neighborhood was so safe, and we lived so close to everything, I would walk oftentimes to and from my favorite pastime: school. School was such a compelling love I would get up early just to get ready, and even during the summers I would ask my teachers for books to keep studying. Assuming all my neighborhood loved school just as much, even more since they all suggested we play school, fake desks were set up on one of our driveways, each supplied with pen, paper and workbooks, and any other books I could find as well. Since it was my turn to be teacher, I stood up and started talking about the first subject, asking questions and suggesting we all open our books to certain pages, just like the teachers at school would do. Everyone just sat there looking at me, not getting excited at all. Finally John said, 'we don't want to go to school, we just want to pretend.' And as he stood up to leave, so did the entire class. My hands wrapped themselves tightly around the binding of the book as I stood confused and now alone. 'Why wouldn't everyone want to learn more?' my little mind mused. 'That is really weird.' I left the books as well, joining them in a less interesting game.

This failed schoolhouse happened a couple years after a life changing event when I was five or six. The day was sunny and it was my favorite time of year, autumn. Why? First of all, we were back in school and my new pencil box (a decorative, cardboard cigar box) smelled crisp and boasted brand new scissors, pencils, erasers, and a specially chosen sharpener. The first week of school gave me syllabi of every subject for the whole year with all its promises of new learning. Walking home on this day remains etched upon the senses. The air was crisp just like the smells of school supplies, and the temperature was beginning to drop, making it seem a little chilly. All the leaves were turning bright colors of orange, red, and yellow and many were already falling. The scent in the air tinged my nostrils and the wind picked up randomly, swirling the leaves that had already descended to the ground.

Movement. The movement was palpable, revealing a dance. Ah, nature seemed to be in a swirling dance.

It was quite impossible to resist joining nature in its revelry, so I would whirl and whirl all the way home on days such as these. But this day, it would be different.

My feet whirled around the corner, down the cul-de-sac towards home, stopping in front of our neighbor's house by the sudden desire to take it all in, in complete stillness. Breathe; my body breathed it in like a thirsty person gulping water after having gone without for days.

Slowly my eyes scanned the world around. A leaf across the street caught my attention as though it had spoken out to me, 'look at me, here I go,' and it gently broke from its branch, fluttering towards the ground. At this moment I have no idea how long or short the following series of revelations took place. The leaf orchestrated the turn of events. While words to describe the moments come easily, they are a step away from the wordless encounter. At first, when the leaf broke and began its descent, I was feeling the joy of the dance. But out of nowhere, deep within, sadness and grief arose. I felt really sad the leaf broke away from the place where it was living, for it was going to die. Then the feeling arose, 'Is *that* what life was about. Was everything just moving towards death?' In that very feeling, time seemed to stop and a veil pulled back on the leaf beyond any thought or feeling. Effortlessly, a knowing came. The leaf was IN God and God was in the leaf. I was IN God and God was in me. All became luminous and clear. THAT is what life is about, 'becoming in God,' and nothing will ever die, or cease to be, but all things live and become IN God. Sheer happiness cascaded throughout my soul and all sadness was wiped away. I wanted the whole world to feel this kind of happiness. In that moment, I acknowledged that I would not have a 'career' other than being and becoming in God and sharing it with others.

Nature was not the only consistent gateway for the experience of Divine for me, even if its pristine setup is void of the limitations humans construct. Ritual proved to be just as powerful. The songs, the prayers, the fellowship and the Communion all formed my young psyche. In addition, my grassroots catholic parents modeled a life devoted to true prayer, kindness and honesty. In these arms, I drew greater benefit than shortcoming in the house of religion. It seemed failing in charity marked the only times my sister and I would be held accountable by mom and dad. Kelly and I were typical in our sibling squabbles, but we would compensate and make up for it with gifts and even created a short lived plan to dedicate Sundays to imitating the older sisters who lived together on the TV show called, "The Waltons". These sisters were sweet and demeaning to the point of saccharin. You know the fake sugar taste that is too sweet for your mouth? To make up for any time we fought we would try to be overly nice on Sundays. I remember one time standing outside the car and the two of us kept trying to open the door for each other. 'Oh dear sister, let me open the door for you,' I would say. 'Oh no, please, you get in first,' Kelly would respond. And so on we would go until ushered into our seats by external influences, namely mom and dad.

Even earlier influences upon my young spirit abounded. My grandma Braun passed away of breast cancer. She was only forty nine years old. As a three year old, I can remember being with her about a month before her death. She looked like a light bulb as we walked to the bathroom, me holding her hand to help her. Spending these final moments with her was of the utmost important. At the time, I really thought I was helping her. She was filled with light and something in me could see that her body was sick but another part of her was not sick at all. So I was not sad, not until years later when moments in my own life left me wondering how different it could have been if she could have held me. My dad and I knelt at the communion rail after her funeral. He turned to me, 'Kimmy, do you know where grandma is?' 'Yes, she is here and she is not here, she is in heaven,' my words blurting out without a moment's reflection. I wonder what he felt then, to lose his mom, especially with the tender love she had for him, when he was only twenty five years old.

Like a true grandma, she guided me in that moment. Her very transition broke the physical boundaries of my heart, and without realizing it, helped form a reality where the non-physical was JUST as real as the physical. Is there a greater gift that can be given? Even now, though my hand would wish to hold her hand, there is stability between us, a steady channel where leaning upon her gives me strength.

Timeless moments, as I call them, would happen spontaneously throughout my years, as I firmly believe happens for all children. It was only later, once I defined it as life in the Spirit, that I would seek to cultivate them but while young, I did what young people do: lived, dreamed, and played. My insatiable curiosity would lead me to want to understand what was happening, which might have been unique, while others may let those experiences bury themselves in the back of the psyche. From that pivotal moment of the autumn leaves, all my inner drive was caught up in this one adventure of inner discovery. Even though formal education would complement the inquiry and the monastery would give me a structure in which to experience it without distraction, all life proves to be the teacher.

Seven years old. Recovered from a second broken arm, tonsils out, brownie turned Girl Scout, it was a time of first communions and new bikes and starting to fit socially in school. About this age, Friday nights became our family pizza night, the best night of the week. First of all, my parents let us use paper plates which meant no dishes and we got to drink coca-cola, our one special time to have it! Those childhood days preceded the many Quick Stops offering a cornucopia of sparkling, high fructose, caffeine-laden beverages. We would spend the evening together playing games or watching some Disney program. It seems I usually got to go with Dad to get the pizzas, which was my favorite part of the whole night. Dialing the memorized number on our rotary phone, the order was always the same. 'Two large pepperoni pizzas,' my mom would say, 'for Braun.' Counting the minutes, the order only took twenty to fulfill and we lived about five away. Dad and I would jump in the car to get the cherished meal. The pizza shop was bustling with other families waiting for their pies, kids fidgeting and asking the same questions over and over, 'Is that us? Did they call us? When is our pizza going to be ready?!' Sometimes the line would be out the door. Waiting didn't matter much I could watch the other kids running around and the parents trying to keep everyone calm, while the aroma of pepperoni and fresh mozzarella billowed out onto the sidewalk. Then, our name would be called, 'It was us, it was us!' I would jump up and down as Dad paid the man and reached over the tall counter (which would probably reach my waist right today) for the super large flat boxes. Once I got in the car he would put our meal on my lap and the heat would bear down upon my legs. Dad whistled his way to the driver's seat and I would have torn emotions of either wanting to just drive around for hours with the pizza sitting on my lap, warming my knees and causing my nostrils to tingle from the pepperoni spice rising, or drive as fast as we could home so that we could have our special meal together.

That was the usual run of events Friday nights, but this Friday night turned out a little different; Kelly was chosen to go with Dad. 'Ahhhh,' my heart sank, but only for a moment, because immediately I thought, 'I can set the table and make it extra special for when they get back!' So I did. As best as a seven year old can do, the plates were placed, a fork on the left, a knife, blade inward on the right, 'Yes, that's the way it goes,' my thoughts rolled. The napkins got the special fan-fold even though they were paper and each set delicately upon the middle of the thin paper plate. We had glasses that said 'Coca-cola' on them and were shaped like an upside down bottle, so I put them out and filled them with ice. 'Mo-om, where is the coke?' I shouted and she disclosed their storing place. Feeling confident, I used the bottle opener myself without spilling a drop. Slowly, ever so slowly, I filled each glass so the foam would not go over the top. Not knowing to tilt the glass, only a smidgeon of the dark bubbly substance could hit the bottom of the glass at once. The ice and the angle catalyzed an explosion of foam. So slowly, ever so slowly I poured and waited, poured and waited. 'Each coke would be nice and cold for our dinner,' I relished. After adding in some crayon colored centerpiece, the table was set! It was all so exciting.

I went to the living room to play but after a few minutes returned to the table to see how things were. To my dismay the glasses were beginning to sweat and drip onto the table. I wiped them down before the water reached the plates. 'Oh no,' I exclaimed quietly, 'I set the table too early and they are not home. I ruined everything!' The thought was a sinking feeling into discouragement. Something quite unique happened. As my heart felt like it was sinking, a hand seemed to immediately catch it and time stopped. Knowing followed, just like the autumn leaves, I had not failed. Our joy as a family wasn't dependent on how well the table was set but rather because we were together. Relieved of the inordinate responsibility my limited perspective had put upon my small shoulders, the night turned to magic.

With my mom and dad involved in Christ Renews His Parish, a charismatic renewal form of retreat and bible groups, we grew up familiar with prayer, ritual and gifts of the Spirit such as lying on of hands, a form of healing prayer, prophecy and speaking in tongues. My first communion fell within this time. The religious lessons fade as receiving Christ in Eucharist felt like an obviously natural thing to do. 'What was there to learn about receiving God?' I wondered. After all, we are created by Him and Jesus was here to unite us all. A boy named Jimmy was my partner. My dress had bell-cupped short sleeves and white on white polka-dots, and the veil we bought was simple. Other than the special feeling of going shopping with mom the dress mattered very little to me. In those days, the Catholic Church was just making the change to receiving Communion standing with a gold paten placed under our chin as a safeguard to catch the Host if it did not make it from the priest to our tongue.

There was a delight in having a partner, a man walking beside me, even if I already had plans to marry our parish priest when I grew up. 'I love him,' my parents would hear over and again. 'I am going to marry him when I grow up,' confidently informing them ignorant of the two most important details, that he was celibate and he would be about thirty years older than me.

Walking up the aisle at the time for Eucharist, everything around me became blurry. The body lines of my schoolmates seemed to blend with the colors and the movement and it all felt like sea-like waves moving in swirls of gold and white. It was a really cool feeling. As the priest placed the consecrated Host upon my tongue, all my body felt like I was floating, moving into the subtle dance of color around me. The lightness imbued me with joy that went beyond my body, and I had no idea how I moved from the priest to my seat. Somehow, it just happened. My eyes could not express the level of joy within, though I tried by looking around to meet other glances of joy. 'All my schoolmates looked so reserved and calm, how were they doing this? How were they so cool and collected when it took all I could do not to jump up with joy?' I marveled. How I admired them as I constrained myself with the prescribed decorum, working hard to hold in the pent up joy.

In the parish hall, the basement of the church, we all ran around like rabbits, showing each other our gifts, playing tag, and eating cake. My parents gave me the most beautiful rosary; the white pearl beads luminously took on different shades as the light cast upon them. It was housed in a silver glistening case with blue velvet lining.

Soon after the reception, I took the rosary to our small grotto where a statue of Our Lady of Fatima and three more small statues of young visionaries were enshrined. Most of my hours there were spent ignoring the short iron fence that separated the scene from the people that wanted to pray. They put the kneelers outside the scene to protect the statues and I suppose to also create a sense of reverence for the historical event. Feeling so close to Mary, I would always jump right up onto the ledge where Mary stood. Still excited, I told my friend, 'I promise to say four rosaries a day!' while balancing a few flowers in crevices of her crown and elbow.

More promises poured out of my mouth, ones that would soon be forgotten but well intentioned in the moment. Imagining what it would be like to pitch a tent and sleep right next to one of the statues of kneeling children, I thought the joy would stay like this if only I stayed as close as possible to Mary.

This definition of sacrament, 'all elements of life are potentially or actually an instrument of grace,' came to me in my graduate studies, giving credence to experience where every intention can open to know that all life happens for our highest good. This was shown to me in fourth grade, during a moment of rejection.

A friend and I were walking around the playground chatting away like happy chickens, oblivious to everyone around us. As we crossed near the hopscotch games, two schoolmates, Sandy and Valerie, began walking behind us. It felt uncomfortable immediately, but I had no idea what was going to happen. So we walked a little faster, but not fast enough to get away from a swift kick from Valerie into the back of my knee. Buckling but not falling, we both walked faster. Another sharp kick landed on my leg. My friend went untouched and as we rounded the corner almost running to get away.

Everything became a blur as my friend dissolved from my view and I was shoved against the wall near the dumpster. A handful of girls had quickly become a gang, all pushing me. The flurry shrouded the faces aside from one or two, as I was kicked in the head and in the stomach. Sadness, shock and confusion forced me to be looking around trying to know what was happening, no disagreement or fight had been a precedent, no discernible reason came forward as my memory grasped for reason. At the same time I felt completely safe, there was this knowing that nothing could really hurt me, and alongside the confusion sat calmness. The end moment was the one most compelling, a couple girls pinned my arms out to me side and two little girls walking by looked at me, 'Look at her, she looks just like Jesus!' they said. These were the only words I heard or remembered. As they said it the presence of Christ flooded my body, we were together in the moment, it wasn't like He was 'there' with me, and it was like *we* were 'Christ.'

Inside I felt strength, strength enough to forgive them without them even saying they were sorry. Life was clearly much more than surface events, and even though I was too young to hold the wisdom of these many realities, at least I could see the truth of their existence. This painful moment was also the most consoling that year for me. Somehow the two seemingly different qualities, one good and one bad or hurtful, coexisted, intermingled, and showed up within my story.

There has been incredible evolution in my understanding of such happenings in the world. At that age, I sunk into the Christ reality for it felt true and felt good. In later years it would seem that I was given an honor to be united to Christ and then at another time it would seem that Christ was there for me in my suffering as a compassionate friend.

Now meanings matter much less as a source of security. I do not feel as much a desire to understand the transcendent meaning of situations, for even what my mind might perceive will still fall quite short of the immense orchestration of life. Let us simply act, and *be*, compassion, honoring the full range of human emotion and experience. Living an open ended question of Spirit so that what we are meant to 'know' will reveal itself free of all our limiting judgments.

CHAPTER TWO

Sunny Days

It's much harder than I thought
or maybe I didn't think at all

Cascades of thoughts
rushing like the spring melt
of an icy mountain
vainly seeking…
racing too fast,
again

NOT LONG AFTER, IN fact the very next year, my family prepared to move to Florida. With my mom loving the sunshine and new environment and my dad able to fulfill a dream of being a fireman, our yearly vacation spot, Sarasota, Florida, became our new home.

As a little girl, it is with complete ignorance I say our move was seamless, but it felt like it was easy. Selling one house, buying another, changing jobs and schools, my parents were only thirty and able to manage us and a new adventure.

One day, towards the end of fifth grade, I was sick with a flu running through the school and lay limp upon the couch with the 'throw up bucket' beside me. Dad was in Florida while Mom was working things out as we finished school. 'Diiiiinnnnng-dooooooong, diiiiiiiiiinnnn-ng-dooooooong,' the door bell beckoned me off the couch. 'Da-yad!' I yelled as he happily stood before me, 'you came home!' He and Mom decided to surprise Kelly and me with a visit. But the big surprise was still on its way…

Mom had come home from work, and the two of them sat on the side of the couch as Dad handed me my birthday gift. I opened it like my favorite treat was waiting inside and saw a small white t-shirt with a picture of an Indian on it.

Trying to be grateful for this plain t-shirt, I remembered that the real gift was to see him again. They saw my look, but secretly new their plan, waiting a little longer before revealing the real birthday surprise. 'Well,' my Dad began, 'we were just thinking you might want to try on this shirt now….since…..' he paused looking at me with that glint in his eye, and mom sitting by hiding her excitement to keep the surprise, I was clueless.

'Since…' my Dad hung out on that word until it hurt a little, 'since you will be going back with me next week to Florida to live!'

'E-e-e-e-e-eeeeeeh! Really??! Really?!' my thrill exploded, this was the best birthday gift ever.

And we left. There was an unexpected blessing that came my way in the move as well. My parents had found a school for gifted kids to learn together. It was a unique program designed to give children of all ages a place to move at their own pace of learning. The school required not only a certain level of I.Q. but also self motivation since the system utilized as little standardized schedules as possible.

Mrs. Frantz, one of the founding seven innovators of Pine View, still orchestrated all the testing. I spent days with her, hoping to be chosen. 'On the borderline,' she told me, 'your tests put you on the border of acceptance and we have decided to accept you!' The new home, Pine View, gave me a place I could be myself without criticism. It was the hand of God reaching in to care for my emotional well being.

Around this time I started reading the Bible out of curiosity. Lying in my room my fingers would randomly open to passages, talking to Jesus about them, asking questions, giving my thoughts back and inevitably praying into the night.

I began to reflect upon the devil, not an entity I believe in anymore, but back then I did believe there was an angel who wanted to *be* God, instead of being an instrument of the power *of* God. It made sense because it modeled what humans do, so if we do that, misunderstand the nature of power, then certainly angels do it too.

My feelings became really strong one night when praying. Filled with love I told God, 'I know, I just know that if Lucifer could experience your love he would want to be with you, I would even go down into hell to love him so he would know you if you wanted me to,' my words rushed into my room.

My room became this place where blue light seemed to show up; I had no idea why except that it felt great, like God was visiting me even if it was my imagination tacking on meaning. But things did happen in that room. The next year we were celebrating my confirmation at Islands of Adventure and the Disney theme parks and I hurt my arm going backwards down one of the flumes. Laying there in a sling the first night I began talking to God, 'I don't want to have to go to school with this sling, how will I carry all my books?' teasing my Divine Friend. 'Can you heal me?' I asked Spirit. 'Show me prayer can work for me as well,' I went on humbly but confidently. Something inside me knew, just knew the prayer would be answered. A light from the foot of my bed appeared and void of fanfare my arm was completely healed. This realm without time or space was more like a coming home to a natural part within me and seeded the ever growing pull to a life of prayer.

The experiences also satisfied my early childhood longing to travel with the speed of thought. For long periods of time I would wonder, 'how can I think something and not do it at the same speed? Or move there at all?' It seemed to me that the contradiction was due entirely to my not being whole yet. My eight year old resolve was that human beings were meant to travel at the speed of thought; we just did not know how to do this yet.

Years sped by in Florida with all of us toasty brown from the year round sunshine. We always found a way to make it back to Cincinnati to be with family, though. My parents were models of showing up in life never allowing busyness or cost to be a reason to skip supporting family.

One year we returned to see our great grandparents. Kelly and I grew up with four in our midst as children. My grandma's dad on my Dad's side, and my grandpa's Dad on my mom's side, and my grandma's mom and dad on my mom's side all lived into our junior high school and high school years. This particular visit three of the four still alive had all moved to nursing facilities.

What a difficult change it was to see my part of my family moved from their own homes to a place for constant care. We went on one visit to see my great grandpa Wilson who was my grandpa's dad on my mom's side. I think it was the only time we saw him before he passed.

'Wow, preh-teee nice,' we all commented as we walked into a plush foyer with overstuffed couches, rich floral prints, carpet so thick it felt like we were bouncing as we walked, and soft free standing lamps. 'I am so glad he is in a place like this,' we all bubbled lightly, looking forward now to seeing him in this new home.

The deception hit us like a bomb as we rounded a corner and headed down his wing. Out of sight of the entrance the carpet stopped abruptly, like it was holding a rebellious refusal to cross the line to the residents. Cheap aluminum molding sealed the edge of the plush décor, and the floor turned to linoleum. The walls turned white and the lighting changed to obnoxious fluorescent tubing running in long continuous strands before us.

What was even worse was the smell. The air was filled with stagnancy and sadness causing my heart to sink. We walked down the corridor counting the numbers, 'two hundred one, two hundred three, two hundred five...until we came to his room, two hundred thirteen.' I drew in a big breath, 'we are here for him.' The mantra played in my head until we saw him laying there helpless and immobile. The light was in his eyes but all the rest seemed out of his control. Fear rose from my stomach moving through my chest and shoulders and up into my neck. The fear was so great to see him at this point that vomit was not far away. 'I need to go,' I pleaded in a whispering tone, and they nodded briefly without turning smiling eyes from grandpa.

Anger at all these people made my body shake as I walked out of the sterile hallway back to the empty designer couches. 'These residents matter. And they are trapped in that dismal wing having to call it home.' I felt powerless and guilty. Powerless because I could not do anything for my grandpa and the others committed to live out their days in that ugly wing. Guilty because I was terrified at what my great grandpa's situation represented. Again end of life leading me to death looked me in the face. This time I was not sad, I was afraid and sickened. 'Never, I never want to be stuck here like he is, but what could I do?' my thoughts ran rampant as I bridled, still feeling bad for not being strong enough to go beyond the smells and limitations of his last home.

The honesty of my real thoughts allowed a small crack in my heart to open with light. This timeless moment happened much more seamlessly. As I stood before the fear a small sentence came forward from deep within, 'fear is not reality. If I have fear, then I must not be *in* reality.'

Peace restored my calm.

With peace came an inward promise. 'When I am old enough,' I told God, 'I am going to get a job in a nursing home to get *into* reality.' Still in seventh grade the fulfillment of this promise would have to wait three years. But true to my word and clearly convinced the direction was Spirit led, my first job was with the Sisters of the Poor and their nursing home of eight floors.

Serve it enough to say that my first weeks working at the nursing home were a sensory challenge. Changing dentures and toilets, giving baths and helping to feed were only a few of the aroma filled tasks before me. My stomach would revolt as the aging of these bodies hid the wisdom of these souls. But I knew. I just knew if I could persevere by being patient, not with them but with me, reality would break through. And it did.

It happened with a cantankerous old man who not only needed extreme care but was not particularly grateful for assistance or helpful in letting us know what he needed. Standing near him one day cleaning his dentures everything changed. Sitting in his wheel chair he looked at me with a glint in his eye and said something incredibly revealing and wise. Like Helen Keller understanding what water was, the veil of illusion was broken and in poured the glorious reality for which I pined. The whole of who he was with all the depth, personality and history rushed upon me in tides of revelation.

From that moment on the job became a love affair. No longer was I bound to the superficial repugnance of aging bodies and culturally conditioned disdain for growing old. I could finally see their beauty, their wisdom, their simplicity. And my preference was to be with them more than anyone else in the world.

Fear does not show reality.

Fear such as this is a veil. Period.

Some worry arose within me in my teens. An inner battle set in motion as I began to wonder what it really meant to be 'free.' The music of the Doors and the poetry of Jim Morrison fell across my path. His deep voice resonated with my desire within to break through to the other side. The crux of my dilemma was passion and spirituality. 'How do they fit? Most spirituality taught a wariness of passion but I felt so passionate for life and pleasure, and isn't this of God too? Can I be passionate and spiritual?' The conflict was not resolved with ease.

Nightmares were my lot. Confusion filled my days. Each time I acted on passion guilt followed, even if the passionate expression was socially acceptable like being enthusiastic. But it was the core meaning of this question that rolled around within, wrestling to understand each other. Outwardly no one would have guessed I walked around in emotional pain and constant scrutiny, 'Who am I? I want to live life fully! Is it okay? Or will I be a 'bad' person? I love people and seek to serve; I must be okay, right? What place does personal sexuality, or drive, or any sort of passion fit? Is it all relegated to lower realms of the psyche?'

Migraines and depression and an inability to ask anyone for help ensued. I wanted answers but did not know what to ask anyone.

This dark night lasted three years, three long years. Then light broke. Pure grace broke open every broken thought and feeling within me. *I was loved into existence. All of what I am is a gift of God.*

CHAPTER THREE

Love Calls

Standing again at the edge of a cul-de-sac
Standing at the edge of consciousness
I am born into embrace
My very arrival is into the arms of existence
and there I am fondled and nurtured
> *there I grow*
> *there I fly*

Yes, I have traveled the world
> *present to ALL*

Everything changed. Every. Thing. Changed.

With Augustine of Hippo I could say, 'Late have I loved you beauty ever ancient ever new, late have I loved you! You were within me but I was outside, and it was there that I searched for you. In my unloveliness I plunged into the lovely things which you created. You were with me, but I was not with you...

Created things kept me from you; yet if they had not been in you they would have not been at all. You called, you shouted, and you broke through my deafness. You flashed, you shone, and you dispelled my blindness. You breathed your fragrance on me; I drew in breath and now I pant for you. I have tasted you, now I hunger and thirst for more. You touched me, and I burned for your peace.' *Confessions X.27*

It was a good thing. The evening it all happened was January 10th, 1987 in Santa Cruz California. The utter freedom of what actually happened is shrouded in mystery. The effect was a feeling of being picked up out of my mire and being brought home. The intensity of that inner darkness, even the pattern of thoughts intertwined with it disappeared forever.

The insight showed me that it is not possible to be *out* of the embrace of God only out of the awareness of that embrace. The consolation brought me back to the dance of autumn and the falling leaves of the five year old little girl. But I still needed to go home to be with my family, to sift through the three years and undertake deep personal excavation and healing.

My Dad and I stood in my room about a year later. 'You are really creative,' he said. 'Do you want to stay here and go to college?' his voice did not hide his desire for me to stay. The deep love coming through broke my heart for within I already knew California was my home. Holding his tenderness like a delicate flower, hoping my words of leaving again would not let it go I said, 'I am not sure why Dad, but I need to go back to Santa Cruz something about being there is home for me.'

The moment was bittersweet,

Yet, letting go allows our life to unfold naturally.

'This was just like the years of Camp Marydale when little Kimmy would run off for the adventure,' I reminded Dad. The reason I could be an explorer was because the love of him and mom were my anchor.

Days and nights a continual communion, 'yes my Love, yes to you, yes to all, yes, yes, yes.' All the other pieces of life were just details. They organized themselves like ants effortlessly moving mountains.

God pursued me. It felt like a courtship and I could not get away from Him nor did I want anything else. His hand was upon me, his heart bled into mine, and my soul sang after him. Hours of meditation and silence were a coming home, a making love, a peaceful after hour of basking in the stars of the universe of this new world.

From the age of nineteen to twenty three this courtship and honeymoon phase lasted, unraveling me in its constancy of love. Every time Mass was offered there was a rushing feeling through my body taking me somewhat out of this world, or straddling me between two. 'Take this, this is my Body,' Christ said it through the priest as tears literally poured down my face. One time the knowledge of being loved forced me to repress sobs as I made it up to receive the Eucharist. They were uncontained after that, 'It is you,' my heart swooned, 'it is you.' After receiving I was unable to move from my seat. 'She is having a direct experience of Christ,' one girlfriend said to those gathered around me.

Walking into any church where the Eucharist was housed would plunge me into this same rush. Usually I would fall into a seat immersed for long periods of time. Seeking did not exist. I would not have even known how to open myself to Spirit in this way; not a word, nor intention, nor did steady practice open these doors. God, God alone opened these doors.

Love called me catching me in the bidding to kiss me on the lips. The kiss took me across all horizons into angelic realms. Day after day this was my bread, week after week life grew into a lifestyle where silence and meditation was the matrix from which all work and play happened. All activity became a creative expression of the uncreated place of my abiding.

My roommates in Santa Cruz introduced me to St. Francis Shelter and man named Paul, the founder. Paul's eyes were birds in luminous flight framed by a nest of wiry brown hair and brown beard. His clothes were donated and the only distinction between him and the people staying at the shelter was the ring of keys to open the doors which he wore with a little embarrassment. That is until he spoke. His words set him apart giving you a glimpse of his wise, unpretentious, childlike soul. No one would have guessed he had formerly been in a corporate money making lifestyle.

Immediately I began volunteering at least one day a week. He invited me to join him and a few other friends in a small mission chapel for a practice called Lauds or morning prayer. The prayer was part of the ancient Liturgy of the Hours, a rhythm of devotion using psalms, readings, and prayers recited or chanted at set hours of the day. The practice carried the celebration of Eucharist into daily life. 'Who knew?' I thought. 'All these years of being catholic no one ever mentioned this prayer existed.' Ed, one of Paul's friends, showed me the full four volume set which followed the liturgical year closely, and explained how they use the abbreviated book where all is contained in one book. Not long after I had one of my own.

Paul would open this quaint chapel about 6am. It was a mission chapel hundreds of years old. The doors were thick wood with iron hardware and set in a white stucco arch framing the entrance. The same humbled feelings arose every time I opened the doors before dawn. Pulling the heavy looped handle as softly as possible my muscles would flex with the weight and I would quietly step over the threshold into the dark. Three candles flickered animatedly offering a hue of color into the space as their golden glow fell upon the painted statues and old canvas tapestries. One light was in front of Mary. The bottom parts of her upward gazing eyes would look pooled with tears because of the angle, giving her a sense of being in awe of object of her gaze. She was either taken by God or thought the ceiling was fantastic. The second light was in front of the old wooden painted tabernacle sitting in the center of a Mexican style iconostasis. The last light sat in front of the statue of St. Michael the archangel. I always found myself kneeling on the St. Michael side of the church.

Utter silence. We all knelt there in the dark utter silence. The silent group communion was the greatest thrill I could have imagined. My dreams were being fulfilled right before my eyes. I was free to open to rushes of Spirit, deep prayer, or even plain uneventful abiding. There seemed no better way in the world to spend my days in service than these precious moments.

After an hour, sometimes two depending on whether Paul had opened the doors at five for us zealous souls, the lights in the sanctuary would go on. One by one we moved like dollops of ice cream, converging from our solitary places to the two benches on either side of the altar.

Ed would usually set us in motion after books were opened and parts were assigned. We sang an opening song, chanted three psalms, read a reading, offered intercessions and then closed with a prayer. With quiet decorum we arose once finished and made our way through the heavy doors into the bright morning sun. All the introspection gave way to joyful laughing hugs. Day after day we immersed and emerged, immersed and emerged.

St. Francis' shelter was an advanced place to volunteer. Paul publicized it widely and community seeking helpers could sign up for a year or two at a time from anywhere in the world. If someone wished to receive shelter they were required to live the rhythm of the group which included social activities and night prayer. We also had copious resources to offer residents training, certificates and degrees. Having switched to a community college for my own education gave me the chance meeting of Pedro one of our shelter guests. 'Keeem, Keeeem,' I heard a voice calling to me across campus; it was Pedro who had stayed with us for a couple months. He ran up and we held a long embrace, 'Keeem, I just got my degree,' his eyes glossy, 'and it is all because of you, I never would have done this without the shelter's help.'

Cheryl, one of our visiting volunteers taught me a great lesson. She was dying of cancer but when you looked at her all you could see was a golden glow. One evening as we walked upstairs for night prayer I asked her, 'how do you have so much joy when you know you are going to die soon?' She responded ever so lightly, 'The cancer? It just is.' Such wisdom came to me through my short stint at Paul's shelter.

My dramatic mystical experiences led me to questions. They felt clearly of God, but what if they weren't? What if I was just deceiving myself? As a twenty year old girl I decided to look around for a mentor or spiritual director. It was to no avail. No one understood what was going on as I described it and every meeting left me feeling pain or frustration. One priest, highly recommended to me, was a spiritual director at a monastery. 'Maybe he will understand,' I thought with hope.

'Hmmmmm,' he gave a long pause as I shared the rush that would go through me and how it took me into a place of ecstasy. 'Are you sure you are not falling asleep?' he gently probed. 'No, this is just the opposite,' I anguished, 'it makes me feel even more awake and alive.'

With that meeting I gave up trying to find advice from anyone. Affirmation was not long in coming my way. One evening lost in communion hours before the evening Mass, Mary's presence came alive in the statue before me. I was praying the rosary, a traditional Catholic prayer. My sense of self disappeared and I dropped into silence which filled my body with sweetness. The top of my head felt like it opened wide as buckets of sweetness gushed into me. From there as at other times I went where the experience took me. Today it took me into Mary. As my mouth strove to say the rosary without sound a soft, round 'something' kept rising in the back of my throat. As the words came forward this round 'something' came forward and out my lips with incredibly strong fragrance. Each bead the same thing happened. At first I had no idea what it was then it came like a lightning bolt, 'roses!' Each bead was a rose coming from my throat out my mouth and into the world!

Sleep was deep that night filled with people alighting around. In the morning my roommates and I hung out for a while. 'I thought you might want this book,' Tom unassumingly yet fatefully said. He handed me a black and white paperback book entitled, 'Autobiography of a Soul,' by Teresa of Avila. 'Who is she?' my curiosity piqued. With the morning off work I took my new book and nestled in bed to enjoy a read.

Her words fell on me like rain upon an open land. She shared her experience of God and it was like a balm for my lonely soul, 'Yes! This is it, I am not deceiving myself. She has a love affair with God similar to mine!' The book was devoured within days. My first Carmelite friend had introduced herself. 'What *is* a Carmelite anyway?' I wondered. 'Why had we never learned about them?'

The next week another roommate Chad handed me another fateful book. It was *Story of a Soul*, by Therese of Lisieux another Carmelite. My hands got hot just holding the book so once work was done I set up a nice spot in the living room to read. The words arose like fire from the page setting into my heart like a branding. Unable to put the book down page after page her message came to me. It was deep into the night when the final page was turned. Not only had I read the book in one night, but I could quote almost anything from it, it became something of a Bible to me. Where Teresa was my leader, Therese was a soul mate friend. With her I shared my days and my nights, my quandaries and my victories. We were similar in playfulness. At the time she was an incredibly popular saint and novenas abounded invoking her intercession. The first time I picked up one of the small holy card novenas to her was at the shelter. 'Hmmmm,' feeling a bit spunky, 'Therese let's play.' I prayed the novena and in the blank space for you to state your intentions I said, 'How about two roses....one yellow and one pink?'

Three days into the novena was my normal day to manage the shelter. I had graciously accepted Paul's invitation to take on one night a week after coming clear on my own uncertain feelings. First I felt incompetent. I was so young and we had a full shelter of every age range, and strict policies around drugs and behavior towards each other. Could I do it? The second fear was getting close to all the homeless. I was afraid of that level of intimacy, would I be okay? In the question the presence of Christ revealed that drawing close to others through compassion carries its own strength and safety. I could imitate Him. Longing to be close to my new friends in every way, I even bought a foam mat to sleep on at home.

Mouthwatering aroma wafted my way from the three foot high industrial metal pot filled with our evening soup as I opened the back door for my shift. All it needed was a little tending so I stirred and tasted a wee bit, and stirred a bit more. All the volunteers knew what to do so I just pitched in here and there to keep us on track.

A knock came from the side door. 'That is strange,' a puzzled curious feeling arose inside, 'no one ever knocks before time.' So I peeked out. 'Can I help you?' it was an older homeless man. 'Yes,' he started, 'this is for you.' And he handed me a yellow rose!

'Alright Therese,' I chuckled; 'now you only have a pink one to bring.'

Our dinner went status quo, the dishes were quickly cleaned and we all sat down to play a game. Patricia, a quadriplegic woman sat next to me. She was spirited and confident, a true joy to be around and a long time friend of Paul's. Leaning over she handed me a pink rose, 'Here you go.' Then she grabbed my face, one hand on each cheek, and pulled me to her planting a big kiss right on my lips, 'and THAT is from Therese!'

It was no surprise to learn there was a city named Carmel just below Santa Cruz and that my roommate Laura grew up there. 'You know, there is a Carmelite monastery there,' Laura started, 'and it sits right on the highway next to the ocean.'

'Do you want to go?' I asked. 'What if we took a weekend hike too?'

The plan fell into place for the weekend of Pentecost. Laura drove as my mouth drooled all the way down Highway One until the pink marble castle of 'Carmel by the Sea,' poked its tips through the trees. My heart swelled with desire at this virgin entrance into a monastery. The soft marble and limestone created invitation and separation, fortress and abode. The architecture was traditional with a long processional aisle, statues on either side, mural behind the altar, and a side wing with a grille where the nuns participated without being seen by us. A grille is the term used for the frame that creates a literal and symbolic separation between the nun's cloister or residence and the public. Usually it is some sort of metal grate constructed so they can fully see and participate in Liturgy. The same idea is used in the room where nuns receive visitors as well.

Laura and I sank deeply into quiet as our knees descended upon the padded kneeler. Not long after Mass commenced with a Benedictine priest clearly contemplative himself. His presence faded as God came through his words as though speaking just to the two of us. Heat ran through my body with every word. We were not on a time schedule so Laura and I lingered a long while Deep while the rest of the assembly noisily visited just outside the big entrance doors. 'Let's go,' we both looked at each other wordlessly. It was time to get into nature. We wove our way through the din of the joyously chatting crowd joyously when our steps halted to see someone breaking through the crowd trying to get to us. To our surprise it was the Benedictine priest! 'Please, please promise you will pray for me,' he took me into his full gaze as both of us blushed. What better sign could I receive than a direct request for prayer from a contemplative priest?

During this time David came into my life creating a choice between being with him and going forward with being Carmelite. From the moment we began a relationship my inner peace was shaken. Something in me believed he was much holier than me, and his desire for me must be a better indication of what is of God. It was an odd sort of reasoning but there was something for me to learn from here.

Through him I learned about the University of Steubenville, a place where charismatic gifts and joyful service abounded without reserve. So I applied and stepped back into a degree program. Life in the Spirit was the way of life. It was here I could learn to trust my own experience of God within and step back into connection with my deeper longing to be Carmelite. With my new support, and this loving man across the Atlantic Ocean pursuing his own education, I could let go of our strained relationship.

Courage came to place the fateful call to his residence in Rome but the call needed to happen. Sitting on my dorm floor my fingers dialed the international code. It took time for the Italian man who answered the phone to find him but eventually he answered. Running with excitement to get to me his words were out of breath, 'Kim it is so wonderful to hear from you!' His joy made the call so much harder. 'David, I am called to be Carmelite, I know for sure, I….I am so sorry,' my words stuttered. 'I love you, always, but I am not in love with you.' Sobs came from the other end of the line, 'I love you,' he affirmed. And he did, he loved me with all his heart and soul. At the end of the phone call unshakeable peace was mine. When true to our path, peace is our fruit.

From here we come full circle to the lesson of Spirit coming through Elijah…

SECTION TWO

In the Bedroom

I move God in God
Swelling and swirling
Surging and succumbing
I move,
    I move
Seeing and sweeping
Sipping and Slurping

The sips turn to slurps that turn unabashedly to gulps
Gulps lead to wide open mouthed laughter and loud sonorous chaotic dance
Gulps turn to chokes bringing tears and temporary retreat

And I move like a symphony and a monologue
I move God in God

AUTUMN CAME AROUND ONCE again.

Another autumn ushered itself in. My nostrils tingled with changes in smells; my skin tingled with cool breezes swelling and quelling, eyes tingled with multi-toned leaves giving one last flash before they move on… This autumn framed the first letter to the monastery of the brochure Fr. Bernard had laid into my hands.

Days that felt like years brought the fateful letter from them, 'Why don't you come visit us?'

'They invited me to visit!' shouts to my family rang through the small summer home on Lake Cumberland. So Dad and I prepared to drive after Christmas.

The temperatures dropped below zero as we headed west on New Year's Day the final leg of our journey. It was the Feast of the Mother of God, what an auspicious day! The sunshine made the roads bright but the temperature was still about 20 below and my dad's car could only direct heat in one direction. We had to alternate heating our feet and defrosting the windshield. At one point ice formed on the *inside* of the passenger door. I found it quite exciting but am not sure how my Dad really felt; he sure was a trooper. Though the inside lacked comfort the outside made up for it as the land opened wide in every direction. Ice glistened on every rock and bare tree creating a virtual wonderland.

By early dusk the car approached the monastery. The building looked like a hen sitting upon her eggs in deep pure white snow. The unencumbered stars reflected upon the white land making it possible to actually see the monastery in the dark. The property ignited magic and a certain peace, like a familiar old song ran through my body. It felt like coming home.

The inside looked like it had been designed in the 1950s which was not very appealing, but the warm hearted caretaker Earl whose eyes seemed like large blue puddles of water, made up for the stagnant feeling. After showing us our bedrooms he led us into the speak room to meet the leaders of the community.

A speak room was the formal place for visitors to meet with the nuns, usually the leader or the appointed door greeter. There was some sort of division between the two parties sometimes a large window with a grille and sometimes just an open window. My first impression left the hairs on my arm tingling; the leaders' tones were so firm and authoritative. It was a stark contrast to the collegiality of my family, friends and world around me. It felt strict.

My family was down to earth, and kindness was the hallmark quality taught to us. My mom and dad always regarded the three of us (Adam came a bit later,) with equality. They were parents who not only took care of us but also asked us what we thought or how we felt. My school reinforced this level of equality. Pine View was a school for gifted and we were encouraged to question life. To add to this formation my life in liberal Santa Cruz, California, created a worldview where hierarchy was seen as a questionable structure which could lead to misuse of power. I was also in a place of wanting to learn from those experienced like the leaders sitting before me and from the lifestyle itself. This balanced the discomfort around what would feel strict to me. Reading Therese's life gave me a glimpse of the purpose of a life of obedience, and dreams abounded deepening the sense of Carmelite life and its school of initiation. One dream was very interesting. I was in a classroom and a large group of Carmelites were standing before me in a formation that looked like they were having a group picture taken with three lines standing on sequential steps.

There was a Carmelite unfamiliar directing the lineup of nuns. Therese who was standing on the middle steps looked at me and said, 'Remember you will encounter the entire world in the monastery.' This might sound a little confusing but my understanding was that we are all human even men and women in a monastery, and we bring the whole of our humanity wherever we go as we grow and transform in God.

The next day came and I made my way to chapel for the Morning Prayer at 6am. Using the side door of the sanctuary to get to the chapel I could see directly into the choir section. The choir is the section of the chapel used by all the nuns where they can be heard but hardly seen. One by one the women filtered in, wrapped in silence. One nun wore a white veil so I knew there was at least one woman that would be a novice like me if I entered. The white veil is worn up until simple vows are taken. When you enter you receive a modified veil, a brown skirt and brown vest. The first six months or so you are considered a postulant. Once that period is over, a decision is made about continuing. If it seems right to you and to the community you become a novice. This is an intense year of formation. It begins with a ceremony giving you your religious name and involves a deep commitment to your own growth and preparation for vows.

After a year of novitiate the woman decides, always with the community, whether to take simple vows. This is a three year renewable commitment where she takes the Habit, a term used for putting on the garment and putting on the life. At this time temporary vows of poverty, chastity and obedience are professed. The ceremony is a marriage to God and uses elements of the ancient ritual of the consecration of virgins created around 100 AD. Even though these vows are only for three years, the intention in the heart of the nun is one for life. There is a lot of truth in the statement that the vows are tried on for size. The only way to feel vows is to actually be in them.

Since the simple vows ceremony is a marriage, a wedding dress is worn. Unlike traditional weddings where the Bride enjoys the gown through the reception, during this ceremony the gown comes off halfway through the ritual. The woman is left standing in her tunic in front of everyone as a living symbol of being divested. Before she is clothed in the Habit her hair is cut off which is incredibly moving for all present.

Checking out all the nuns as they entered it was clear to me the community was a full range of women. Most communities had one or two around my age still in formation from which the age jumped ahead about 20-30 years. Not long before I had visited monastery in the northeast and felt a deep connection with the leader. She was kind, gracious and exuded wisdom. Even though she was excited about the prospect of my joining them, she also felt the five of them might be the final nuns of that monastery. They were unable to keep the traditional hours like younger women would understandably desire. Her acceptance in life felt so loving

I wanted joined just to learn from her. Desire for a traditional schedule was too great, just like she predicted.

The chanting softly broke the silence. All sang in unison, creating one voice with many women, lulling me into its sweet cadence. The stanzas throughout rotated from one side to the other and back again. The very action of facing front then facing each other felt like an embodiment of transcendent and imminent. They turned towards Christ in the Eucharist then turned towards Christ in each other tossing the sacred words back and forth like a ball of light.

I wanted to be part of them. Desire to join them in common hopes and dreams, common prayer and intentions welled up during this pre-dawn ritual.

We would be hard pressed as humans to identify only one motive for any choice we make. There may be reasons we claim as conscious and we may even say it is an answer to our prayer. Even when we acknowledge prevailing motives, layers dwell within and below our choices. This gives depth and texture to our journey revealing life's mysterious quality. It bows to the transcendence of Source always drawing creation forward in good. In this mystery there they stood, twenty women chanting and bowing.

The second meeting with Mother Maria Teresa and Mother Anna took place around 10:00 am. 'Our community made a commitment back in the early 1970s to keep our charism revolving around prayer and meditation. We love to chant,' they went on proudly, 'and have preserved ancient chant in addition to writing our own.'

'Yes!' I thought. 'I hit the jackpot here.' I quickly pulled my guitar out of its case and flipped to favorite song of worship from Steubenville. Strumming and crooning, I full-heartedly sang a song of praise to Jesus. They looked at each other as though I could not see, 'well....' The sub-prioress Mother Anna said coolly yet sincerely, 'you *do* have nice resonance in your voice.'

Buckling at the reservation I wondered what it would be like to be in a strict community. Would it feel like my spirit was squashed? No way, strict or not, was right or wrong only a matter of discerning individually what would be good. What I did note was that I was very young and had everything to learn. Asking for a sign was my means of resolving the decision. The sign came a few hours later. During evening prayer a novena card fell out of a book into my amazed hands. It was the very prayer card I had been using for months to help me find my new home! Decision made.

The weather jumped during the night from 90 below to just zero degrees. Dad and I laughed our way to the car peeling off layers like it was summer. We talked and talked. He had a pretty good impression but wanted to know how I really felt. Layers of implications were before me in the answer causing a long pause. Finally I said it, 'I think this place is it, I want to see about joining here.'

Arriving home my letter asking to be accepted into the community was put into the mail.

CHAPTER ONE
Days and Days and Days

Go with me,
    Let us run upon the mountains
    and gaze upon the valley
    Let us fly over the canyons
    and swell up to the highest peak.
    Capture the vistas with a sweeping turn of the head as though they were
blades of grass

Go with me,
    running into open fields of wildflowers
    smelling the presence of loved ones passed
    opening our hearts to all we do not know

My hand longs to hold yours,
to pull you with me, and feel your pull in return

No limits, no more.

MY SENT LETTER PUT me into a state of expected waking. It was like holding a vigil candle and gazing deeply inward each moment. Each time I turned outward became a chance to return inward. I waited, and waited. 'How long do these things take? Should I call at some point?' my patience was tried easily in those days.

Yet the longing was one of tremendous humility. My hope was that my yes would meet a yes which would mean much more to me than some sort of accomplishment.

One rainy day as we drove up to the post office, 'You wait here while I run in,' Dad jumped out the door at the same time. As I sat there a sweetness washed through me and I clearly heard these words, 'Arise my beloved and come, for the rains have passed and the flowers have begun to bloom upon the land. Arise my beloved and come.' (*Song of Songs*, parts of Ch. 2) I knew. I knew the letter was there and it was a yes.

Sure enough Dad jumped into the car and pulled the letter from the pile, it was a formal yes.

The invitation was to enter on the Feast of Our Lady of Lourdes, February 11. This was the birthday of my grandpa on my mom's side and only 4 weeks away! They were breaking a normal observance by letting me join days before Lent was to begin. Lent was a time of extreme fasting and lots of special practices that might jar a woman new to the life. They thought I could handle it okay and didn't want me to have to wait until after Easter. The list of what to bring was small: white nightgowns, boxer style underwear, long black stockings, twin size sheets and a few pencils. It took me more time to give things away than to fill the list. The white nightgown was a source of consternation though. Every store boasted every pattern imaginable: spots, stars, hearts and stripes. The colors were bold as a rainbow without one option for the plain white asked of me. I devised a scheme to buy the lightest patterned one I could find and soaked it for hours in bleach. The effort was to no avail.

We decided to have a Liturgy and reception at the Notre Dame Convent close by my grandparents' house. The retired Sister Magdalene and I had hung out in the grotto chapel many days. She had taken my cause into her own hands, storming heaven as a fellow bride of Christ. Through her the use of the church and hall happened with a simple phone call. Father Bernard and many Steubenville friends came down to celebrate Liturgy. Even my dear friend Michelle took lead guitar for the charismatic songs that would heighten the celebration. The church and hall were packed.

As in ages past good friends from my parents' days of Christ Renews His Parish hosted all that had traveled. Stomachs full from their traditional sausage egg casseroles and fresh fruit, hearts full from hours of sitting and sharing we lingered. Marcia with her spunky sense of humor and Jerry with his quiet yet light filled eyes created a living embrace uniting happy childhood memories to the day.

My feelings were really mixed. I even felt a little irritable wondering why I was leaving all this beauty. Then clarity would return reminding me that the beauty was coming from the celebration of becoming Carmelite. The last moments with Kelly were, in some ways, the hardest. We would not be raising kids together. I would not be there for her physically and she would only be able to visit occasionally. Hope that we would stay close through the silence weighed heavy on my heart. As we drove to the airport so she could fly home to Florida we hardly spoke. A hug let us say all that could be said.

Not long after taking my sister to the airport the day of my departure came like the tide that comes in swiftly without notice. 'I'm not ready, I need more time,' my senses said. But I was more than ready. They were typical human doubts coming in the face of radical commitment and change.

The early Kentucky morning came upon us. My mom and I hugged goodbye before she had to go to work and my Dad drove me to the greyhound station. He was not going to stay because he didn't want to see me go. Silently I hoped against hope that his feet would not move until I left. 'How was I going to do this if I did not feel him standing there waving goodbye?' I held the wish without imposing it upon him. The last thing he needed was for me to ask even more of him. He stayed.

'We have to go now, time to find your seat,' the driver said, not realizing the implications of this statement. My heart sank to me feet, I could feel the rush downward and the emptiness that followed. Yet my feet moved to the call of my spirit. After my arms let my Dad of so much tenderness go, these feet, like a strong friend, turned me around to climb the two steps that felt like thirty. They carried me to a seat where I could see him. 'I could still turn back, I could still leave,' the thought arose, but for years the Carmelite life had beckoned to me in surges of love and desire. So I trusted and I surrendered and I let go.

My Dad stood there, courageous and vulnerable. I sat there courageous and vulnerable. The bus moved. Starting slowly, gravel crackling under the wheels, the large vehicle made its way out of the parking lot and sight of my Dad faded like a mirage.

Sinking into the seat thoughts ceased entirely. My eyes took in the open land from the highway but they did not contemplate anything. Poems did not well up within. Emotions laid still and quiet. And I just sat. The scenery was not magical like the drive for my first visit, but it was not barren either. It just was. And I was. This one memory would remain all my days; it captured the stripped serenity of my soul.

A man was on the receiving end of my journey, just like the beginning end. Earl carried my bags and ushered me like a queen. Soon my few belongings would be merged with the community. I wanted to be poor just like Jesus. Everything about his life that was recorded or attributed formed the ideal for my own life. Poverty seemed a straight path to richness of soul. The leaders were clearly happy to have me yet kept their calm reserved exteriors

Sister Mary John was the complete opposite. She could not contain herself. Speaking under her breath, her silence broke like little bubbles burst with a pin, as we laughed our way through the measurements for my postulant skirt.

A last phone call to my family was scheduled for the night before my entrance. My mom, dad, sister and I all sat there on the line. What did we talk about, really? Nothing, we just hung out as long as we could. Lingering over the line let us feel like we were in the same room. The hanging up was laborious. My hand did not let go the receiver until they hung up first, even then I held the phone to my ear imaging they were still there. Replacing the corded hand held receiver into its base upon the wall was another action of letting go erupting into feelings of sadness. It took the evening to let the feelings go and return to the serenity that had marked the sojourn to North Dakota. Sleep aided everything and I awoke with excitement over the pending ceremony.

CHAPTER TWO

Immersion

Stretch yourself into a new wineskin
    today, today
Wiggle out of the old useless scaled membrane
    today, today
The covering protects you not
Save to deprive your lips the taste of your ever new way of being
    And the finest wines to spill into gulps of your ancientness

Toss your head back so the night can fill you with its wine
    Be drunk with me
And we will run in the moonlight spinning and tossing
Laughing ourselves into waves that ebb and flow
Constantly changing
Becoming unchanging
    Today, today

MONDAY FEBRUARY 11ᵀᴴ, 1991. I sat plainly in the front pew of the chapel spattered with a couple handfuls of people attending Mass with me. Did they know what would happen today? Did they come out to support the sisters gaining another for the fold? Or did they just show up for their daily ritual of attending Mass? Regardless their intentions they would be participants, willing or not of my entrance taking place before the end of the Liturgy.

The first reading was from Isaiah 66. 'You will be carried upon His Lap and will receive everything in heaven,' God's promised through the prophet. This feast day marked the appearance of Mary to Bernadette of Lourdes, a young, uneducated girl in France. Bernadette died on April 16th the very day before I was born, which made me feel like there was some sort of transference of mission that connected us. My thought was of Bernadette passing me the torch to carry on the love of Mary. Bernadette's life had the consolation of appearances of Mary to her in Lourdes, France. While her body is incorrupt, her life was bereft of earthly consolations. Growing up poor no one believed this little girl's mystical experiences at first. Mary would have her do very eccentric sorts of things during the apparition like eating dirt, which only added to the skeptical disbelief. It was only when dramatic healings began to happen in the waters there (the spring was hidden until Bernadette showed everyone the source,) that she gained some respect. All along she had to trust that her own experience was true. Her strength of soul must have been tremendous. And now God alone occupied my own heart and mind as I walked towards the grille. Strength like a steady moving ocean swelled within me.

The days of courtship ended and here we stood ready to commence the next stage of our relationship.

The priest called me forward to the front of the large grille now wide open. Two nuns stood there. One I recognized as the prioress Mother Maria Teresa and the other was the novice mistress, Sister Gemma. She would be with me day after day but I had not met her during my speak room visit or my preparation days leading to this step.

Standing there it started. Laughter started rolling in my belly until it flew out of my mouth. Of all things I stood there at the threshold of the cloister laughing while everyone else stood in amazement! I think I even slapped my legs with my arms. The entrance words formed some kind of background noise to the ensuing joy, 'The waiting was over…I am really going to be Carmelite!' Excited, shaking, nervous, disbelieving and yet ecstatic I was raring to walk over the threshold to my new home where equally excited and yet somewhat baffled women waited to greet me. Soon enough it happened and the large metal grilled closed and locked behind me. Each sister waited to greet me as I was led by the novice mistress around the room. My arms flew open wide offering big bear hugs to the nuns trying who were desperately trying to practice modesty by taking only my elbows in return. The sister closest to me in age was so excited we began to jump a little together as tears welled up in her eyes and giggles, yes giggles, escaped from her throat.

Everyone looked the same. Seriously. Not only were the habits all the same color, but for some reason the looks of peace and joy in each face shaped into the same likeness. It took me weeks to begin to discern differences and about a month to be sure I did not mix up a couple of the sisters who had the same body type.

I was shown to a place to stand and we processed from the choir to the refectory where we ate breakfast talking freely. Processing was our way of walking in formation to and from chapel. Talking freely added to the nuns' excitement since monastery meals were normally eaten in silence with one sister reading. The awe of being with them spread through the meal and took away my appetite as I watched and watched

Processions tied the moments of nuns' lives into one continuous prayer; a symbolic movement taking us from one activity to another as a group. I loved processions from the moment my first steps joined. They were not new to me. In Therese's autobiography she speaks of them. In one passage she talks about a procession while chanting a psalm. In the distance she hears the din of a party going on in a nearby mansion. The faint noise was a cacophony of music composed of multiple streams of chatter and laughter that reached high pitches of squealing and low echoes of baritone. In that moment she reflected upon the silent walk she was taking from the choir helping a cantankerous nun to the refectory. Her heart was filled with gratitude; nothing could be as satisfying as this walk for the love of her Jesus. Nothing would compare with our many days and nights of walking side by side, chanting psalms as a single voice as we moved to and from choir.

When we left choir that morning the prioress gave a loud knock on the wood stall where she knelt. Everyone then kissed the kneeler and rose. The nuns were divided directly in half so each had a partner on the opposite side of choir. The youngest nuns were towards the front followed by the next in line. Youngest was by entrance date not chronological birth. The line extended all the way to the back where it stopped with the prioress and her assistant. They had their own kneelers side by side in the center to make it easy to see and offer direction. When we left the youngest led and all followed forming two side by side lines. When we recited or chanted verses alternated from side to side just like the Liturgy of the Hours. Once the first pair of nuns reached the front they genuflected together and moved to the door. We would move through the halls side by side reciting and praying. The living symbolism ignited my passion; we were literally a moving prayer of the Divine. Here I learned the helpfulness of hierarchy, to give direction so all could concentrate on other more sublime things.

Once we reached the refectory (the place we ate) everyone moved to different places. Some of the sisters sat with older ones they helped serve and the novices all sat together at one table. I was to learn that while this did not matter much in silence, when we spoke it made it easy to talk with those with whom you lived and worked. More prayers were offered before the meal. The nuns took turns leading the prayer in and out of choir. When the prayer finished everyone bolted in different directions. It was almost as though we were in a huddle and when done we clapped into action everyone moving to their post with speed.

Once I was assigned roles, like taking the covers off the pots of food, my whole body would fly into action just like my sisters. It was almost involuntary. Many times monastic life felt like a symphony and this was no exception. You could liken it to a smooth flowing symphony movement going from allegro to adagio to scherzo. After the prayers ended we were all scherzo...maybe a little schizo! Then the community lined up at the service dishing up in silence. I was completely baffled about where to go, stand, or sit so the Novice Mistress nudged me along. After all were seated the prioress would normally ring a small bell and the designated sister would begin our spiritual reading, but not today. Today the bell was followed by joyous voices saying hello.

The structure of the lifestyle was very childlike. We were eager for the moment, excited for the small things and willing to trust, or try to trust, our process of surrendering. The complexity of the world can make living on this level difficult and isolating.

Breakfast ended all too soon and the tinkling bell silenced the bubbly current of voices. The feeling of joy was too palpable to cause the abrupt change to feel abrupt. This would not always be the case sometimes the move into silence would feel like loss or lack, all depending on the inner state of the moment. The silence would be a solid consistent ground to cultivate my ability to observe myself with kindness. The kindness took longer to develop than the skill of observation. At first it was pretty easy to observe all my weaknesses and hit myself over the head with internal words of judgment.

Silence magnifies the movements within because of the empty container it creates. The empty container offered space for another path to grow, the path of compassion.

Silence revealed to me that most of us have a dualistic attitude when it comes to compassion. Towards others it can flow quite generously while towards our self it can be hard work to offer this kind of gift. Sadly many Scripture passages have been easily interpreted to reinforce this self directed sword with the words, 'Off with her head.' Ultimately love dissolves fear, and fear is the real culprit.

In a complimentary way silence offered me new vistas of understanding others. In silence facial expressions, unexpected body movements, looks of sadness, all stood to be misperceived if you held onto your own interpretations. Here there was a blank slate to learn how to receive understanding of what was really happening for the one before me. Vistas of compassion and intuition opened.

As we left the refectory Sister Gemma quickly made her way to me. She guided me away from the main current of nuns walking towards what I would soon learn was the dormitory for solemn professed nuns. It was the south end of our U-shaped monastery. On the north wing was a door set on an angle leading to the Novitiate. It was a quaint wing with three rooms on either side of the hall and a room with a window laden door at the end. It was sweet and old fashioned. We walked directly to the door on the end into a large room adorned with pictures and statues. An old, crackly white, wooden pipe organ was the first object to jump out at me. It resembled something that would be in a circus with its animated carved wooden details on the corners and the large padded pedals requiring steady pumping to move air into the pipes.

Sister Gemma's first words inaugurated our relationship. She straddled something between friend and superior. Gemma was charming, warm and intelligent. She was short and her manner was somewhat shy at first and quite dramatic once she opened up. She raced through details about schedules, prayer books, novitiate duties, bathroom use, rules around writing home, my cell, and bedding instructions crunching the information into a quick half hour. I remembered a little of it, somewhat distracted from the big change, and emotionally surprised to learn just then that my family could only receive letters from me every six weeks.

A novice mistress is the principle contact for a new aspiring nun. It is to her you turn and she holds the place of a superior for you, taking upon her shoulders the responsibility of teaching you the life.

We slept in rooms called 'cells.' While many, perhaps you are among them, think of prison this is far from the reference. We drew upon a Carmelite, Nicholas of Narbonne, who wrote *The Flaming Arrow* around the 13th century. In this text he refers to our eremitical lifestyle lived in community to be like a bee hive with each one of us occupying a cell. In our cell we gathered the Divine Honey. It was a perfect fit for the lover in me which has always been one of my fundamental archetypes. Understood here in my new home, encouraged to 'give myself to the Beloved' without reserve, there were no limits but the ones I laid up myself.

My cell was closest to the Novitiate classroom and faced the open grounds. The room seemed to be about 10'x10' with a concrete floor and bare concrete walls. There was one large window letting in plenty of light. My furnishings were incredibly simple with one four foot high free standing unit that had four shelves for my clothes and the sparing books I would be given to use. It was plenty of space but I marveled at how my whole life would be lived with so little. The white painted metal desk was just large enough to put a piece of paper and lean your elbows upon it to write; and the wooden chair with its slightly uneven legs and bowed center offered the simple service of a seat. The final piece of furniture was my home made bed. The frame was made from 2 low sawhorses and two large wooden planks upon it. The mattress, rising high like a mound of dirt, was a cloth ticking with a large vertical slit on one side into which corn shucks had been stuffed until not one more would fit. 'How fun was this?!' I thought.

Sister Gemma and I headed back to chapel for Terce (midmorning prayer,) and the sister next to me showed me a full shelf books in front of where I was standing. They were all for me! Chills went down my spine at the love with which they were prepared for me. There were so many of them. The four volume Liturgy of the Hours with a respective

1500 pages each, an older abbreviated Liturgy of the Hours with side by side Latin and English, a Carmelite supplement hosting the feasts and memorials of all those in my Order throughout the year, a small homemade prayer book used after meals, the magnificent Liber Usualis, a 2000 paper thin paged book of Latin chant for the entire year, revised and compiled by the Monks of Solemne in the late 1800s and lastly a binder holding all the special arrangements of chant, some written by the sisters themselves, for daily and special use. There was an entire stack of pages that could not fit in the binder and I could quickly see that all the pages would need to be changed quarterly.

These were the principal books we would use. There were other books too if you can believe it. My favorite cover was made by Sister Mary John. It was a homemade binder with a yellow vinyl cover that lasted me to the day of my departure ten years later. In this binder were all the hymns and songs we sang for Mass. There were quite a few from different cultures. We even had the original German version of Silent Night. We also had a Lutheran hymn book with all the old standards like, 'Holy God we Praise Thy Name,' and a few other less used hymnals.

'My own library in church, now that was kind of cool!' I reveled. Our schedule was one of the compelling reasons I chose this monastery. This was one of the only communities still getting up at midnight. The Latin phrases marking times of prayer designates the Liturgy of the Hours. Following Judaic tradition of stopping to pray during the day, these hours were a continual extension of Liturgy. The word Liturgy means both act of God and act of the assembly which is the body of Christ. Our primary dedication was to be this outpouring in the heart of the world. With the Council of Vatican Two religious communities were encouraged to examine their observance and return to the simplicity of their roots or charism. This monastery chose to keep contemplation front and center, taking the risk to let everything else happen around the schedule of chant, prayer and meditation. This choice required most of the work to be done in small windows between Terce, Sext, None and Vespers. It was a sheer miracle to see it happen. When necessity requires it is surprising how actions can streamline. After only a few months I could get a floor swept and clean our Novitiate room in just five minutes! Accomplishing what was asked in the way it was asked was seen as a grace of obedience, and it became a playground of continual surrender and daily miracles.

Here is the schedule of my particular monastery:

Midnight	Matins (Vigil prayer of meeting the Beloved in the night)
6:00am	Lauds (Morning prayer, hinge of day, praising the dawn)
6:30-7:30	Meditation/Mental Prayer
7:30	Mass
8:30	Breakfast
9:00	Terce (Midmorning prayer)
9:15	Class for novices
10:00	Spiritual reading
10:30	Work
11:30	Sext (Midday prayer)
Noon	Dinner (main meal)
12:30	Dishes etc
1:30	None (Midafternoon prayer)
2:00	Work
4:00	Class for novices
4:30	Vespers (Evening prayer, hinge hour, bringing day to close)
5-6:00	Meditation/Mental prayer
6:00	Supper
6:30	Dishes
7:00	Recreation
8:00	Compline (Night prayer)
9:00	Bedtime (to arise at 11:45pm)

I was completely lost during the 15 minutes of Terce. The sister next to me sang the starting hymn from one book, quickly re-filed it while opening the second volume of the Liturgy of the Hours, and flipped from one place to another alternating psalms and antiphons, readings and the short ending prayer. All the while she was bowing, standing, and sitting in synchronized motion as a bodily expression of the ritual. Even standing moved from facing front to facing each other and then back to front. My body moved like molasses as I tried to pick up on the feel of the sister next to me to keep in sync. On top of it being complex it was a workout. The first days of monastic life left my body sore from prostrations, kissing the kneeler, walking miles down the corridors and back for each chapel visit, and all the bowing and sitting. No wonder everyone was so lean.

Like a swift moving stream we left chapel as we entered and everyone scattered in different directions taking up their daily duties. I followed Sister Gemma who motioned to me. We made our way to my new cell. Normally the half hour after Terce was devoted to spiritual reading so Sister Gemma brought with her a book for me to read. 'Ah, I thought we would get to choose our reading!' my heart sank at first. It was no sacrifice however, for she gave me the first volume of a three volume set of early Christian stories. The lives of hundreds of hermits and contemplatives after the times of persecution from 300 AD onward were told upon the pages. Lesson after lesson about silence and virtue and joy and obedience poured upon the page. Even though eremitical life boomed from the time of Constantine (300 AD) up until about 600AD these books seemed to span a wider range of time. Anthony of the Desert and all those around his time, the Stylites, (men who would climb a tall column and live there alone,) the women escaping the expected paths of for them in society, abbesses, monks and the hermits all created an alter world of friends hanging out in my cell each morning.

Sister Gemma was a bit self-conscious in giving me required reading after these three volumes she slipped me authors of great inspiration and interest like John of the Cross, LaGrange and Thomas Aquinas deviating from the prescribed list for new Carmelites. Her classes were brilliant as well explaining a scholastic view of the human person. This is one of many views that fed a dualistic understanding of grace and life. From this theology we have grace a 'gift' coming from outside the human being, the will as a faculty needing to be directed, and our vows of obedience as a 'higher' path for self realization. The community was incredibly conservative even using the old version of the Baltimore Catechism. I remember looking at the picture of a child praying in the catechism as parents were counseled. 'All vocations are holy, but blessed indeed the parents who raise a child called to be a priest or nun. Even if my theological views were different than Gemma I learned so very much from her. She was an adept teacher capable of taking big concepts and explaining them in clear simple words.

We washed ourselves with a pitcher and basin. At first it felt so primitive but soon after took on a simplicity and practicality that was kind of fun. My first clumsy attempts still bring a grin. 'How could I get clean once the wash cloth got dirty after scrubbing the first part of my body?' The impossibility seemed insurmountable. After filling the pitcher with hot water and retiring to my cell we had about ten minutes to get ready for bed. I would wet the washcloth, lather it up then wash as much as I could. From there came a dip and rinse in the basin of water. From there on out I had to continue in baffled fashion with a dirty cloth. No doubt the other sisters must have cracked the code of how to do it better. It took time but soon a strategy evolved. If I only used the clean water lathering the cloth each time and spreading it on me, I could save the rinsing until last. Even though I would need to stay wet and sudsy all of me would get clean water before rinsing. Put shortly, wet and lather my entire body first. Rinse last. Just enough water could be saved to pour over my toothbrush once, brush my teeth having put the toothpaste directly into my mouth, then pour the water over the brush to clean it. This way both my cloth and my toothbrush would be rinsed before set out to dry. Victory!

The first couple nights I went way over time for getting ready for bed. At 9:00pm one night a hand reached into my cell and switched the light off right in the middle of my basin bath! I was wet and naked. I went over and turned the light back on so I didn't get water on everything, but the hand came back in and turned the light off again! It just about brought tears to my eyes I was laughing so hard. So I left it off and went to bed somewhat dirty and partially dry.

Even though entering was exciting, my prayer time was bereft of the feelings of Presence I had enjoyed for over four years. Chuckling I would tease God, 'Here I am finally here to be with you all the time, where are you?' But my soul felt security and audacity in His Presence, not needing the ecstatic phenomena of my early stages of relationship.

The first days of getting dressed were also comedic; it is too bad there were not hidden cameras to record the efforts. With the 5:45am grogginess upon me, my hands fumbled to pull clothes from hangers in the dark and put them on correctly. I had a very hard time getting the veil on even when it was light out. We had no mirrors as well so it was just like being blind. 'Late…I was late…again,' I tried hard to speed it up as a light knock came upon my door. The tenuous rap seemed to say, 'I'm so sorry, please don't feel bad.' What made this stressful was that it did not affect just me, but the whole novitiate. The four women stood face forward waiting patiently for me at the end of the corridor. Each morning we would walk two by two saying the words of a psalm on our way the choir. If one of us ran late, we all ran late.

Rushing still to meet them we started a procession that looked more like a race of rats towards the chapel. We were all late. One by one we knelt in front waiting for the prioress' knock to kiss the floor and scurry to our places. It was my first experience of the 'all for one' in community, inspiring awe for the selflessness of my new friends. We took great care to recognize our mistakes as part of a lifestyle that would help us grow in wholeness. When we made a mistake, we kissed the floor.

Why would such a ritual take the brunt off feeling bad about our mistakes throughout the day? I think it is because it plunged us into a symbolic life in a conscious way. At first recognizing mistakes seemed overly emphasized, but soon the practice became a joyful way to relate to the weak or forgetful parts of myself, it was a move away from self consciousness. Somehow it felt like personal dignity was bolstered, seeing that all my worth was rooted in who I was instead of what I did.

My experience of Christ through my superiors was undeniably the most powerful influence in opening trust to the teachings of the life. The liturgical season of Lent began on Ash Wednesday just two days after my entrance. And one of my most compelling experiences of Christ happened just shy of six weeks later during holy week.

When Ash Wednesday arrived everything changed. The choir where we chanted was stripped of flowers, the alter was stripped of color, the organ was closed, the meals were simple repasts or fasts, and all rich harmony and joyous songs were reduced to simple solemn tones carrying words about Christ's passion and suffering. One of the nuns intoned the first hymn of Lent, 'Au-au-di Be-e-ni-gne-e Con-di-tor.' The deep cavernous hymn effectively launched the forty day walk with Jesus to his Passion, Death and Resurrection.

Every chant through the year had its own sense. The different tones proved to be a powerful spiritual director of my life in North Dakota. The sound opened me to *be* the expression of life, change, death, joy, sadness and every other part of creation. Perhaps it was the hundreds of years these sounds were devotional chanted, perhaps it was the nature of the focus, and maybe it was the hunger of my own soul to really go there.

Gregorian chant and our liturgical seasons were all about story. It was the story of the Uncreated expressing in creation. The more we entered into the story, the more the essence of it could take root in us. Time became quite an unimportant quality of our lifestyle.

The focus in Lent was so exclusively on Jesus it was like having your own private consult, just you and Him. The solitude was magnified because the readings we had revolved around the moments He stood alone. Even though we were living in silence, the quality of the silence took on the story.

Lent held a few surprises for me that did not resonate well at first. One of them was something called penances done in the refectory. The whole concept repelled me for I did not believe in penance. However there is always something to learn from communities that preserve tradition. I set my sight on expanding my perspective.

After Lauds of Ash Wednesday all the sisters clamored to the windowsill outside the chapel. A chart was setup with seven or eight rows each with a different practice, seven columns for each day of the week and a blank line for names. I had NO idea what any of the rows meant other than the holy hour after Compline. For my first week I was told to observe, so I did. Almost all the practices were done during the main meal of the day. As we entered the refectory a sister lightly hit her chest and uttered, 'forgive me my offenses' to each nun crossing the threshold. 'This did not make any sense at all,' I thought, 'there was nothing to forgive.' To an outsider it would have looked like a menagerie of actresses putting on a play with a woman carrying a cross, another fasting, and so on... The cross attracted me though because it most fully imitated something of Jesus' life. The chosen nun started kneeling in the center of the room with a medium size cross on her shoulders, its tail touching the floor. Mother Maria Teresa would knock at some point, at which the cross bearer would kiss the floor and begin to move towards the front, slowly sliding on her knees. Once there she turned left to the front of the tables on that side, then left again moving down the row of tables towards the back of the room. Once she reached the back she would turn towards the other side, creating a rectangle as she made her way up the opposite side of the long room and eventually making her way to the starting point. Added to this, she would stop and kiss the floor three times to honor the three times Jesus fell as he carried his own cross to his death.

What a poetic way to reenact the carrying of the cross and we got to do it every day up until Easter.

Lent let us hold common themes in deep prayer. Themes such as death, loss, betrayal, loneliness, longing for friendship and inner doubt all showed up in our reading and prayer. Sin was also a strong word in my consciousness back then, a way of taking responsibility for falling short of living God's love in the world. As warriors we stood on behalf of humanity and held a healing prayer for transformation in our world, as contemplatives we gave ourselves to embody the call of creation to be one with God.

One evening during our fast which included broth at the six o'clock meal, I made a hilarious mistake. Novices went last and hence could finish any old leftovers sitting out in small bowls with cute little spatulas to wipe them clean. The room was a bit dark but one of the bowls at the end had an indistinguishable whitish, thick textured substance. 'Hmmmmm, this doesn't look like anything we have had at any other meal,' I thought as the contents were scraped into my broth. The goop dropped easily into my bowl dissolving upon impact, and the broth turned a light milky color.

As we all sat at table a knock happened and the sister assigned to reading began her nightly discourse. Napkins were tucked into the top edge of the Scapular looking like bibs and everyone began eating with eyes cast down and ears open. Forks and spoons lightly tapped the bowls and plates. My large soup spoon dipped into the steamy broth bringing the first delivery of soup to my mouth. As the hot liquid hit my tongue fire exploded up into my nose and eyes! Having no idea why this happened I took another spoonful and the same fire spread even into my throat. 'whhhhhhhh, whhhhhhhh, whhhhhhh,' I strove to draw cool air into my mouth without drawing attention to myself. Tears began running down my face and anything lodged in my nose had left by the third spoonful. 'Oh wow…I put an entire bowl of raw homegrown horseradish into my broth!' My mouth hurt and I had no idea what to do. The small piece of bread I had taken was quickly used leaving me without anything to temper the burning through all my canals. We did not have the option to revisit the food table, ever. And we were told to finish everything we took, so I had no choice but to finish this broth. Giggles began to percolate within.

I devised a method of starting the 'whhhhhhh, whhhhhhhh, whhh-hhhhh,' then quickly shoving a spoonful into my mouth midstream, hoping it would ride the wave of cool air bypassing the mouth and throat and make it to my stomach. 'Whhhh-ish, swallow, whhhh-ish, swallow,' slowly the broth disappeared. The sisters beside me were aware but could only give their sympathy through peripheral glances. Recreation, the one time a day we could sit and talk, was the laughing recount of supper. To it were added a stream of similar stories from my other novices and mistress. Simplicity of life bred simplicity of soul.

Would I ever get the gist of our liturgy?' my head and fingers tried to imitate the smooth transitions of the sister next to me. Quietly Sister Perpetua would observe my dilemmas day after day. She would kindly wait until my downward cast eyes darted her way, 'help?!' At this point she would move her book to the perfect angle to see, and lightly point to the page. She was brilliant, knowing when to wait and when to help, without any exaggeration or judgment.

Each woman became an oasis of unique personality and Sister Perpetua was simply brilliant. During recreation she shared the effusive imagination of her mind which was her gift and her trial. Imagine yourself having a fun hour creating silly songs and ideas then abruptly having to move back into silence, while the mind rolled on. That was Sister Perpetua, once revved up she had a hard time calming her thoughts and stopping the creative flow. Perpetua also turned to her superiors for guidance, laying out things she did not understand with incredible courage. It seems she spoke frankly, letting them explain the line of reasoning that accompanies obedience

Weeks of fasting and devotion flew by quickly bringing us to the climax of the Sacred Triduum. This celebration is the most magnificent awe-inspiring event I have ever, even to this day, had the honor of being a participant. The Sacred Triduum spans three days. Those days are called Holy Thursday, Good Friday and Holy Saturday which gives way to the Easter Vigil and the first alleluia of the Resurrection. Holy Thursday begins with the evening prayer called Vespers. The practice of my community was to allow the new sister to be there without any preparation so she could be surprised and what a surprise awaited me. Kneeling there opening my heart I was completely absorbed into the Presence of God. Ah, it felt like the return of a long lost friend as my prayer had been dry for quite some time. We fell into each other's embrace and I heard clearly, 'Draw close to me; I have many riches for you.' The words plunged me into a level of absorption that made it very hard to physically move. Tears poured down my face so profusely my nose began to run and my one handkerchief, quickly soaked by the outpouring, wet my garments. Without knowing how I moved my body and followed the normal ritual of prayer. All those around me moved in a sea of light. Tears continued to pour down my face though I was not crying or weeping. It was the involuntary response of being flooded by the presence of Christ. At one point I made my way to the prioress trying to motion to go to the bathroom. The snot on my face was multiplying by the moment even though I had used every inch of the sleeves of my blouse. She looked at me like I had two heads and denied my request. I don't blame her; I must have seemed very strange.

The prayer segued into a ritual remember Jesus washing the disciples feet. We left choir through the back door and entered the chapter room. This room was both library and meeting room. This first time was a blur of swimming light. As the new sister I was free of obligations which proved rather helpful in the moment given my mystical experience. We formed two lines with the prioress standing at the head. She opened a large Bible to the Gospel of John and began to slowly chant the Last Supper. As her voice intoned each syllable all I heard was Christ, all I felt was Christ. Tears began to run down my face again this time just as copious as the last. It was Him, truly Him speaking. I was there and here all at the same time. No thought such as this came through my mind, no thoughts even existed in those moments, the thoughts I give you are words put to a wordless experience. I figured all the nuns were experiencing the same as me only able to be more composed.

We all sat and took off one shoe and sock, the prioress slowly made her way around the room to wash and kiss our feet. I could feel only Christ in her movement. I saw her, but it was not her, or at least only the shell was her. Once she was to the person next to me Christ's presence was almost more than I could bear. The love was washing through me like waves in the ocean and before I knew it she was kneeling at my feet. She glanced at me but it was a veil loosely hung through which only Christ was felt. When she kissed my foot, it was Him and I swooned backward caught by the bookshelf behind me.

From this moment on I hardly remember anything for days. Since we observed silence from Holy Thursday all the way to Easter I had a safe haven where I did not need to speak to anyone. I walked without walking and sang without feeling the movement of my lips. Meals came and went, and fortune was mine since our fast was rigorous. The two nights of Vigil remain impressed on my memory but I am not sure if I remember this first year or just subsequent years.

Thursday and Friday nights we arose like normal at midnight for Matins. A large candelabrum with about 12 or 13 candles sat in the middle of the chapel for the ritual to come called Tenebrae. Tenebrae is a deeply eloquent service of ornate chant. The candles were the only source of light so each sister had her own small flashlight in order to see the song sheets. We chanted for hours in deep, sorrowful, solemn tones reliving Jesus' betrayal, persecution and ultimate crucifixion. The parts were elaborate and not for the faint-hearted. It was a night to day change from the unadorned phrases of our Lenten chants into a complex array of metaphors and multi-punctum (those were notes in Gregorian chant) syllables allowing us to spread into the looming darkness. One by one the candles were extinguished over one and a half hours until only one lit candle remained. At this point an older sister took the candle out of the choir and we sat in silence. After a few moments the prioress started pounding her stall or seat while everyone else would join in demanding that the 'light' be brought back. The light returned but not for long, once the older nun replaced it in the candelabra she extinguished it. Then a true sadness and loss came upon everything and we spread like oil on water to our private cells.

Good Friday was marked by a six hour stint in choir together from noon until six pm. We would recite Sext after a few pieces of stale toast for our main meal, beginning our vigil with Christ in all the events from the arrest all the way to crucifixion. Along with the Liturgy of the Hours the leaders composed a dynamic rhythm of prayer, music, poetry and silence. A poetic version of the Stations of the Cross peppered the time. Mother Anna had discovered and opera composition of 'The Seven Last Words,' which filled the space with vocalists. Each word was its own tract bringing climactic interludes to the simple somber words spoken in all our prayer. Poetry was read of the passion. Sisters took turns leading decades of the rosary. By the time 3pm rolled around we were steeped in the historical events. We spontaneously moved out to the center of the lying prostrate on the floor as the door for the public opened and closed with our friends coming for the Good Friday service. 'There is no place in the world I would rather be than here with these women.' I never felt such a sense of belonging and purpose in all my life. We were of one mind and one heart just like the Scriptures encouraged us to be. We were like little dots scattered upon the earth connected in purpose.

By the time we all made it back into our own seats the 3pm Good Friday service was ready to begin. Our quiet prayer had imbued the air with heaviness worthy of Jesus' moment of death.

He died. He actually died. Brutally and cruelly handled his death was not gentle like his life had been lived. The contrast of his compassion against the backdrop of monstrously blind circumstances defined his person. He shined brilliant like water that creates a sea of diamonds when the sun sparkles upon it. I thought of all the ways compassion is lived by unassuming people, whose gestures go unnoticed, folding into the tapestry of common daily life void of anything dramatic. This seemed to me just as heroic and just as powerful. It seemed that compassion and integrity are inner dispositions and the real litmus test is not the outer circumstances but the inner canvas.

My longing to be compassion was a life-long dream, first recognized at Confirmation (a sacrament in the Catholic Church.) We all sat around the eight foot long metal framed folding tables in the side room converted from an office into our CCD classroom. It was the budding parish, St. Thomas Moore, still having its liturgies in a linoleum lined cafeteria. We were learning about confirmation and our teacher, Sister Margaret, had just given us a list of saints' names to spark our imagination. 'You want to choose someone who has qualities you wish to imitate,' she explained. As she rolled swiftly into a short intro to each saint's life and what they were esteemed for in their lives, my mind drifted and I had this strong flash of Veronica. The feeling of her pouring her love out for Jesus during his walk to his crucifixion ran through my body and inspired a longing to be like that- not like her so to speak- but like THAT. With sweaty palms and beating heart I blurted out 'Veronica,' when the sister asked us if we had any ideas. The name wasn't even on the list. 'She was there for Christ when others ran away or kept silent,' I uttered, and continued,' her love was so great that she broke through the crowd to wipe his face while he was falling under the weight of the splintery, heavy cross and bystanders were jeering.' I absolutely LOVED her abandon, she could have cared less about the consequences of her actions (she could have been crucified with him for sympathizing,) she was impelled by the movement of love within herself. I wanted to be impelled like that.

Ten years later my life was still caught up in the aspiration, turning to God to create a compassionate heart in me day after day.

The nuns moved into action as the prostration completed. One left choir to make sure the priest had his vestments and books, another opened the and the rest of us pulled out the books that would be used to recall the passion; not long after the service began.

The memorial had three parts each about half an hour long and all recited plainly except for the singing of the Stabat Mater towards the middle. The first part was the reading of the passion using missalettes where all the parts were scripted; the second part was the kissing of the cross and it was here that we sang the endless verses of the Stabat Mater, a hymn recalling Mary standing at the cross. The last part was a liturgy of the Eucharist. The Body of Christ had been taken from the church after the celebration of the Last Supper the day before.

4:30pm came quickly, Good Friday was almost over and we moved into our own silent meditation for a solid hour. The air was thick drawing us into its somber vigil; we were like larvae in cocoons waiting the moment of emergence. There was a repast of a couple pieces of dried toast, 'why did we even bother? It was more torture to have to go to the refectory than if we went about our private duties,' each year I wondered except for this first year for my ecstasy continued unabated.

Holy Saturday at midnight we chanted in the dark with the candelabra again until 1:30am or so. It was a different sense of emptiness than Friday. Friday the loss of Jesus impregnated every element, there was a level of heightened drama from the re-living of the passion, but on Saturday the dust had begun to settle into a feeling of reality that Jesus was gone, he was really gone. The moments would seem to hang on like some sort of gum on a bench, and sometimes I just wondered if we were suspended in time.

Around seven that night we gathered to celebrate the Easter Vigil. What a crash upon the senses! Vase upon vase holding hand cut gladiolas adorned every available surface. All the lights were now turned on to full voltage, there luminosity bouncing off the golden stitched cloths, and the sisters seemed to bounce with each step with confident expectation of what was to come in the Liturgy. I had no idea, and I could not have even imagined what was to happen in the next two hours. The sisters found tremendous satisfaction knowing they had a newbie among themselves, and for the first year it was sweet to see how many of them would look out of the corner of their eye to catch my first impression of the ever changing events of our community life. This evening my heart was ill prepared for the level of exultation coming.

Liturgy began. Not long after a single note came forward from the six week long silenced pipes of the organ. The sounding was followed by a shaky chaplain voice, unaccustomed to singing and moved by the greatness of the moment, 'a-le-e-e-e-e-e-e-ee-ee-lu-u-ia,' he intoned with no accompaniment, officially ending Lent through his quivering alleluia. The sisters grabbed the baton in full voiced unison, every inch of the church reverberated with a joyous release and if the walls could have shaken, they would have.

A moment of grand silence, not lasting long before the pipe organ sent forth another invitation one ½ step higher, and the priest with voice warmed sang a little louder, 'a-le-e-e-e-e-e-e-e-ee-ee-lu-u-ia!' Joy rose and arose within us. We made it, we made it through Lent and the banquet was beginning. Our voices chimed in, overriding his final note as we responded by repeating.

One last time the pipe organ sent forth the single noted call one ½ step higher, causing the joy to build and the priest in self-abandon sang out, 'a-le-e-e-e-e-e-e-e-e-ee-ee-lu-u-ia!' and we repeated at such a quick pace it felt like we were running even though our feet were still.

The organ was the way our Prioress loved to share her joy; her fingers began to move rapidly playing a multi-layered introduction for the Gloria which brought such a smile to each of our faces. We sang and sang. All our harmony parts restored to us after the willing boycott held through the season of preparation. We not only read all seven Scripture readings and sang every single responsorial psalm situated in between each passage this *was* our passion and life blood. You had to love all this to want to be there. If you loved it bliss was your lot, if all the ritual and symbolism bored you, you would not have lasted for more than a month without feeling disdain.

By ten or eleven the Easter Vigil had come to its open ended conclusion, leaving a tease for the following day where the ecstasy would continue. I still feel it today, the veracity of the symbolic life impressed itself deep upon my heart, everywhere I go, I go with these experiences continuing to create perspective on the layers and mystery of life. There are days I wonder where I might find again the quality of living that magnitude of boundless mystery. Sure all of life is a mystery, but most of that awareness is shrouded in the structures wherein we function. Here all of that could be cast aside and we could stand vulnerably in the eye of the mystery without a care. In that place of abandon the transcendent could speak a word of love in our inmost being.

Like the afterglow of a great party, each sister tended her duties with lightness, no one motioned for bed time so I took liberty to check things out and enjoy meandering. Since our private holy water fonts had been empty it was a big deal to fill your bottle from the special Easter water considered to be even more powerful since it was the baptismal water of Christ's resurrection. Long chants had consecrated this water and now we were given sole use of it in our home. One of my Novitiate sisters, Sister Perpetua looked at me with cheeks bright red and eyes glowing. She had a bottle for me and like two young maidens running through a valley we went to catch the Divine water.

The Carmelite charism still remains my own, 'to walk in God's Presence.' With Therese I would gush 'Let Him kiss me with the kisses of his mouth; draw me and we will run after you,' quoting parts of the Song of Songs, knowing that if I was drawn into the Presence of the Divine my very being would effect good in the world; the union would be, by its very nature, an outpouring of service.

And with John of the Cross we all would say, 'I lost all the flocks I used to tend, walking out on the open field, my one ministry is love.' This short line is from his 15th century poem *The Spiritual Canticle*.

Gemma had let me in on one secret before the Triduum; it was the Mary

Magdalene game. One of the Gospels noted that she was the first one to the empty tomb, so the game was to be the first one outside the choir before Lauds Easter morning. The only rule was that the earliest you could get there was 4:30. The winner had to wake up naturally and then kneel outside the door until 6am when we could then enter choir.

It seemed an easy task but not once did I wake up first, not once. I thought for sure I could rally my angels, or even St. Therese to wake me up, but someone else had dibs on their help. This someone else was my closest novice sister, Sister Teresita. She was amazing! She would pull these victories out of her hat with such an unassuming nature; you never would have thought she had such drive (as though anyone could be a Carmelite without drive!) I remember each year waking up with this excitement, 'maybe this year I am the first one up,' and the clothes would fly onto my body as my feet raced me out the door only to see Sister Teresita already kneeling as I rounded the long corridor towards choir. We would all still kneel there, adding an entire hour upon our already rigorous schedule. With Resurrection magic in the air the hard floor could barely be felt.

One admirable sister from the solemn processed wing rounded the corner running, stopped abruptly audibly exasperated to see us all kneeling there, and curtly turned around to return to bed.

Once the doors opened for Lauds we flooded to our stalls, pulling out all the books with the ornate chant that would follow. The chapel still smelled sensual and rich, with notes of incense and gladiolas hanging in the air. Then it came. It was the epic HAEC DIES. It was a one sentence responsory happening just before the Magnificat about half way through Lauds. Its translation was, 'This is the day the Lord has made, let us be glad and rejoice in it.'

With note after note upon each syllable, the sentence was a world unto its own. One time I counted the notes out of curiosity; there were 173 notes for the full version and about 150 for the abbreviated. The line would take us minutes to chant in unison and its movement was an eloquent explosion of joy on whose back we would ride. The very compilation of notes created surges in which the volume of our voices rose until it felt the whole body was singing. We sang it multiple times each day of the eight day celebration of Easter. It was this phrase that opened my understanding of the timeless symbols of Liturgy. Since we celebrated EVERY day of the octave of Easter, we lived the truth that all time is an illusion. If it was 'the day' it would end after a 24 hour period, but this 'day' would last for eight 24 hour periods, symbolically meaning eternity.

My heart sang an enduring hymn of gratitude. This richness of living was exactly what my soul craved; like dry weary land having gone without water (Ps 63) God filled me with delight and prepared a banquet (Ps 63.) The words of this psalm, one of our more popular feast day psalms from the shelter community in Santa Cruz came back for every feast. Bridging time with a memory alive and growing.

Easter spread like a field of wildflowers seven weeks long, starting with the Feast itself continuing for eight solid days. Feasts of word and food accompanied every meal; the Victimae Paschales, an ancient chant commemorating Mary Magdalene at the tomb, added its embellishment to Lauds, and the fasting and weeping of Lent was washed away in the banquet of Easter.

After the three days of absorption commencing during the Washing of the Feet ritual up to Easter morning consolation and illumination were active parts of my prayer again.

The days of courting long past, wherein my being would feel flooded with light, made way to a subtlety of seeing. Passages of Scripture would literally light up before my eyes and it seemed the words would jump off the page as a message. In a few unexpected places God would come upon me like a lover confidently taking his Beloved. One day having finished sweeping and scrubbing the main corridor an ecstatic sweetness rushed through my body like a whoosh. Leaning against the wall just outside the kitchen door for support I could have died in that moment and not even noticed. 'There is nothing to compare to this love,' it was a sense of having experienced ALL.

What would it matter if we traveled the world and yet did not see the flower blooming outside our door? Doesn't the flower contain the whole of the world?

Mine were the flowers.

Spending time sifting through holy books in the front stall one day curious to find new writings, a holy card fell into my lap. The face looked very familiar, 'Oh gosh! It's the woman in my dream with Therese!' The dream where Therese reminded me that I would find the world in the monastery had a woman directing things, it was *this* woman but I did not know who she was…until now. She was the nun who brought the branch of the Carmelites to America years ago. Only now did she make herself known leaving me feeling like my choice had a certain pre-ordained quality.

There was an odd sort of emphasis on Mary and Elijah being our founders by the leaders in our community. They downplayed Teresa of Avila and John of the Cross who came in the 1400s and were considered reformers. By many they were revered as founders since most of the flourishing groups of Carmelites belonged to this branch. Teresa and John had no interest in being reformers they just wanted to live the simple life of contemplatives. In their times the Order had been influenced by the class systems in society and adopted practices that complicated the life. While I loved Mary and Elijah, they had certainly made their presence known throughout my years; I also secretly celebrated Teresa and John. The founder on the holy card has brought the Order not considered part of Teresa's reform.

The schedule of meals was a very interesting experience. Coming from a society that eats its way through the day, the set hours for meals was hard at first. It was a perfect petri dish to notice my own reactions. At first I found myself stocking up by eating large meals and a large snack. The feeling of fear arose around not having enough even though our meals were always grand outside the days of fasting. My hand would load up to alleviate the unspoken concern. 'What am I going to do if I get really hungry and the next meal is too small?! How will I make it?!' Worry abounded. Thoughts of food came to me during prayer. In wondered what we were going to have for the main meal, looked forward to breakfast after three hours of solid prayer, hankered for all sorts of foods we never ate and lamented the 'loss' forever of the over processed, sugar laden American diet that was within reach in the world. During snack time at 3:15pm no one was watching so I didn't have any pressures over anyone seeing me eating too little or too much. It was a hard core lesson in trust as I loaded my snack plate high. Confiding in Mother Anna, the appointed spiritual director, she said most of the women go through the same thing when they enter, and put on a little extra weight too.

One snack time I was craving pizza but pizza was never offered for a snack. 'Uuuuggh,' frustration fueled a resistance to reality, 'I will never be able to have pizza when I want it.' It felt like such a sacrifice, life was about love and now love required me to sacrifice instead of enjoy. I turned all the strength of my focus to observe my body, to notice how it felt as the thoughts ran rampant. In the gentle observation a new series of thoughts came forward, 'Why do I want food to have sway? Do I not trust that I will be pleased with what comes my way? Can I just try letting go and see what happens?'

In that moment I chose the adventure. I let go of all my desires for pizza and the desires to choose what I want to eat and when I want to eat. I love you my God and I choose trust.' The words brought peace and stillness and my appetite was satiated in the surrender.

Work time followed, then a novitiate class. After that came Vespers, meditation and supper. We entered the refectory and the unexpected aroma of tomato sauce filled the air. The covers were pulled off the trays and what lay before me spanning the table?? PIZZA! For the first time since my entrance we were having pizza. On the very day I craved it, and let it go, God provided for my happiness! It was delicious. I noticed the way I enjoyed it was different than if I had acquired it, it came as pure gift. Again silence proved to be a matrix of freedom.

Monastic life with its impelling force of liturgy was a rich tapestry of cosmological color, texture and story. It took years to have a grasp of the big picture of all our rituals, feasts, memorials and more. Our calendar had both moveable and immovable feast days stretching us beyond a rigid idea of time and space. As much as possible we would enter into the living memory and impression of each celebration. The beginning of our year was Advent one of the four major seasons along with Christmas, Lent and Easter. While the world celebrates a lead in to the day of Christmas, we celebrated a Christmas season up until February 2nd. Offering the underlying thread to each year would be extraordinary Ordinary time rich with special days of Jesus, Mary and too many saints to count. Even in the octave celebrations of Christmas and Easter each day had a different dedication. Overlaid this basic calendar was our Carmelite ceremonial with an entire fabric of saints and special days. Feasts of the Holy Innocents, John the Baptist's birth, Teresa of Avila's transverberation, Carmelite all saints, and Pentecost are just a tiny thread of the huge cosmological array of our lives. Words fall short of the all encompassing nature of our lifestyle. The chants, tones and readings would cull the essence of every liturgical day. Our commemorations outside would unpack the mystery even more. For instance, we would watch the operetta, 'Amahl and the Night Visitors' every feast of the Epiphany. We would give and receive 'roses,' a spiritual message from Therese on her feast day. All these elements took deep root within us. Some mornings I would wake up literally vibrating the words and sounds of a psalm. Rather than constrain us through its complex structure, liturgy took us beyond our small human story. Liturgy expanded our hearts to hold all creation. Liturgy opened new panoramic views of Life in full array. We not only enjoyed the tapestry, we became the tapestry.

CHAPTER THREE

Initiation

There is an open cavern within
Sitting still like the starry expanse
Empty with a void, pregnant with an expectation

New life on its way
Stay empty my companion...
Stay pregnant my friend...
The labor pains are soon to start,
unraveling all you thought you knew
desolating all you thought you had

And the laughter of life will soon be sitting upon your lap

During Easter season I was invited to take the next step of commitment. The leaders in the community commented on how naturally I fit in so they asked if I would like to enter Novitiate July 15, 1991. This was just five months after my entrance. The year long period as a novice is an intense time of formation, something like a spiritual boot camp. The intention was to prepare you for your first set of vows called simple profession. Simple profession lasted three years with the choice to renew them, to end them, or to move into vows for life.

'Yes,' simply and straightly I said yes.

The novitiate ceremony would give me my religious name. At this point I would let go of my 'worldly' name that conjured up an entire set of structures. The name would establish a new structure and identity as a bride of God. The world would be my family. Since my particular community was conservative the religious name was considered given by God even if you participated in the choice of names. That meant that you were invited to submit any ideas but ultimately the Superiors would decide. The first time your name would be heard would be during the ceremony when it was bestowed upon you like a consecration. The anonymity and mystery felt exciting to me.

For weeks names rolled around in my head. Nothing stuck. Every idea felt forced or made up. I really wanted to submit some preference so I kept reflecting. One day at my personal holy hour a movement like angels came from out of the blue. Something like a whispering into my ear said, 'Annunciata.' The name had never occurred to me but felt perfect and inspired. As I walked out of the chapel the speaker crackled, 'Buzzzzzzzz, Buzzzzzzzzz, Buzzzzzzzz, buzz-buzz.' Each one of us had a code and this was mine. The buzzes were rarely needed and mine usually happened when I forgot to do something. The sound was an easy way to call a sister wherever she might be in our sprawling monastery.

Quickly walking to the prioress' office Mother Maria Teresa motioned me to the sub-prioress Mother Anna. This older co-founder of our monastery seemed tough in her approach, but the hard exterior was easily broken for those with spunk and confidence. Mother Anna is now deceased but she was really very soft, kind and rather spunky. "Kim, I am putting together the list of possible religious names for you. Do you have any you wish to add?' she asked.

'Are you serious???' I thought, wondering if she had any idea about what happened during my holy hour minutes before. Seeing she was not interested in dialogue I kept it to myself and said quite simply, 'Yes, I would like Sister Mary Annunciata. We paused wondering what I should be 'of.' Most everyone had an 'of' something, like Sister Martha of the Eucharist or Sister Angelica of Mary. Mother Anna chimed in 'How about 'of Jesus'?' and we both smiled.

I felt certain about the name but also felt like it was a gift not coming from me. What an unusual feeling it was to actively participate in the very gift coming to me knowing it was of God.

When the day of the ceremony arrived I happily entered into expecting to receive what was perfect. Who knew if this name would really be given to me so why not expect something wonderful? This is the very name that will be mine for the rest of my life.

The words of the ceremony began and a magic filled the air. With the air I felt myself literally changing amidst the ritual. It felt like all my cells were reconstructing themselves. Kneeling at the grille I listened to our chaplain preside. The prioress and novice mistress stood ready to put the white veil on my head. 'You will no longer be called Kimberly Braun, 'he recited, 'from here on, as a symbol of God's choice of you as his Bride, your name will be Sister Mary Annunciata of Jesus.'

The words rang like wedding bells in an open sunlit valley as tears spilled upon my cheeks in a continuous stream. I *felt* chosen, I *felt* consecrated. The Novice Mistress helped me rise and hugged me dearly. She motioned me to make the rounds to hug each sister one by one. Mother Anna who was still lightly crying, she grasped me tenderly with her Kleenex crumpled in hand. Our eyes locked for just one precious moment.

After my entrance hugs where I threw my whole body into full on embrace, the Novice Mistress informed me that we observe greater modesty in our touch. The practice was to touch or hold elbows and lean forward not touching the body but only brushing the sides of the sister. The veils would lightly dust each other and sometimes the sides of arms would solidly lean upon the other, but otherwise the embrace was empty of any real physical contact. 'Mmmmph,' this was not very fun to put into practice.

To make it fun today I decided to put all my effort into how you can give love without being touchy feely. It was an opportunity for me to focus upon the energy that gets exchanged as we give and receive. Instead of seeing her instruction as a loss I grabbed hold of it as a gain. If love truly knows no bounds why does it need to be expressed in the way I am used to practicing?

The superiors were consistent like centurions standing at their posts. From my perspective they believed in their role as one of service and practiced it with sincerity. Divesting new Carmelites so they might find their true selves was part of that role which made formation intense. Yet even in what felt like severity, sincerity could be seen in their eyes. This understanding cultivated freedom for me to learn and grow.

One of my centurions acted her role in relation to chant one day. As my voice grew stronger so did my volume during chant. Without realizing it I began to sing very loud! My prioress let me know this in no uncertain terms in front of a fellow novice. It hurt my feelings at first to hear her words but upon reflection it was a great chance to learn to listen more closely. In choir I began to apply myself to hearing all the other sisters and add my voice to what was there. In a way it was more self reflection which is what we strove to move away from, but in another way it increased a great skill, that of listening.

She was the messenger not of some external truth about singing, but of an internal opportunity to learn about myself in relation to others.

Still in the wake of becoming Sister Mary Annunciata a real darkness about the life came up for me. First let me confide that the sound Sister

Mary Annunciata rang like wedding bells with enduring freshness all the days of my religious life. Even today fourteen years after returning to Kimberly Braun I can say my religious name with the same sensation running through me.

Speaking of wedding bells, bells in general were prominent for us. They rang for all the important moments of the day. They dismantled the time driven world from which each of us came. Time can be used to organize our lives into increments, where here time was marked by prayer alone. There was a subtle way everything became free.

When the darkness after the ceremony descended and lurked in the corners of my mind time became almost unbearable. I felt restless from the thoughts in my head. Everything about observance outside liturgy smacked as fake and manipulative to me. The word observance defines how a community lives out its charism in the day to day life.

'Why did everything have to be so structured, so orchestrated? Where was creativity and spontaneity? Was I shortchanging myself in staying in this community? Wasn't there a responsibility to develop our God-given gifts? If all is at the service of community, isn't that utilitarianism?' These and many similar thoughts rolled obsessively through my mind.

I was afraid I had stepped into a system that would end up squelching my very spirit. Was this the way for me? Should I stay? Am I failing to be true to myself? Everything was called into question and inwardly storms rolled without abate. My ceaseless thoughts ran in reaction to everything around me. It was easy to disagree inwardly about a perspective or to hold my own counsel but would I be affected over the years?

Was the call of love like a fire in my soul, plunging me into silence and mystical experience a good enough reason to stay?

The dilemma raged in my psyche.

When it came down to it I did not know if I believed in a vow of obedience as it was taught to me. There was not an opinion of something being right or wrong, only the question of what was right for me.

No clarity came. Mother Anna's words of hoped for guidance fell flat and days became sheer torture. From August to January my view upon community life was a skeptical critical commentary.

This made the first Advent tumultuous. Even the charming ritual of transferring the Jesus' empty crib from cell to cell each night lacked luster. The simplicity and the fasting of Advent served as a preparation for new life to come in the cosmos, it was an existential emptiness to be filled on Christmas. This stripped ornamentation mirrored my own inner state of chaos perfectly. The words and chants however were bright with hope and expectation of what is coming. It is something coming into creation that has never been experienced before. Advent gave me fortitude as it presented a joyful pregnancy waiting birth. The season carried me as I suffered myself.

Even in my skepticism my soul was walking a Carmelite path by asking deeper questions. One of my graduate professors used to say, 'there is a fine line between an atheist and a mystic.' It takes encountering our inward limitation, the 'what something is NOT,' to come into a greater experience. In other words, new channels were being chipped away so new light could come.

December 6th, the Feast of St. Nicholas, we sat eating our early supper in silence when a loud knock shook the refectory door. One of the younger nuns, our joyous and spontaneous Sr. Elijah bolted through the door. She dressed in a traditional Santa Claus suit pulling a large cart behind her filled with gifts.

All the silence ended and laughter ensued as she did silly tricks, even throwing in a cartwheel or two.

'Huh, I bet they told her what she could and couldn't say and do,' my mind rolled. 'How fake it all is, it's all just a mind game and poor Sister Elijah is just being controlled.' I feigned a weak smile as my sisters on either side looked excitedly to share the moment with me. I felt terrible to be having these thoughts, 'What's wrong with me, at least I could enjoy the fun with everyone,' I vainly thought.

Anytime I mustered a 'yes' to staying doubts shattered the tenuous peace. Anytime I rallied a 'no' and would decide to leave another legion of doubts assailed me. Mother Anna would leave quotes on my choir stall like, 'God's will gives light to my path....' which was a quote of a psalm. 'What WAS God's will?' my frustration would ignite. Her attempts only added to the fire of confusion.

At a certain point I stopped reaching out for help. It was all useless. My psyche was a broken record so I just did what John of the Cross suggests, 'nothing.' When in a place of confusion, he counsels, do not make a move in any direction if possible. Just wait.

As severe as my inner turmoil was it was unable to cut me off from the utter brilliance of the first Christmas.

On Christmas Eve all hands, except mine, prepared behind the scenes. New sisters were excluded from every preparation so they could be surprised on the day. Flower arrangements, decorative plates filled with homemade goodies, cloths for Liturgy being ironed and fancy vessels cleaned and readied, chant practiced, a life size nativity scene with starry sky assembled in our choir, a music player set up in the refectory, decorations everywhere and so much more created a whirlwind of excited activity.

Midnight Mass came in with a flurry of color and sound, and organ embellished familiar Christmas songs. About 1:30am we all processed to my surprise to the refectory. 'AAAAAAh!' I gasped as the doors opened upon a wonderland with colored lights, music playing and decorations adorning every crevice. Fun springy ornaments hung in our procession path begging a hand to reach up to pull or ring them. They were not disappointed as one hand after another gleefully swung upward to keep the movement going. It was embarrassing to see all the sisters looking at me in my vulnerable awe stricken state. As I gasped, they giggled. Looking to the right was a table with decorative cloths peaking through a mountain of edible treats. Homemade cocoa, cider, butter, preserves and breads wound around plates of cookies, crumb cakes and candies. What joy! What joy! Now THIS was the way to celebrate Christmas. Every lip raced through the grace, 'The Word was made flesh,' began the chantress. All responded in fast paced rhythm, 'Alleluia! And dwelt among us, alleluia!' A few more phrases and responses, an Our Father and the final blessing, 'May the King of Glory make us partakers of the heavenly table.' 'AMEN!' we shouted. The bell rang and with it the cacophony of nuns' voices sounded like we were a party of hundred hungry women. We ate and drank until about 2:30 in the morning.

But this was not the end of our night together. We processed back to choir. Only the lights of the life-size crèche were turned on. A starry sky upon a sheer black screen glistened from the crèche up to the twenty foot high ceiling. We knelt in silence. From the silence the prioress began singing Silent Night. Voices joined one by one quietly revering the mystery before us of Christ born again. It was another Incarnation within our own hearts and souls.

Like Easter, the Feast of Christmas lasted for eight days.

The octave day of Christmas is New Year's Day and one of the largest feasts of the year, Theotokos, Mary, the Mother of God. On feasts like these even our prayer at midnight lasted half an hour longer as we add ancient chants such as the exultant Te Deum. This long rhythmic chant called in all the angels and saints. It was during this vigil that a cloud began to rise from my troubled heart. Just as the darkness came upon me unexpected so the shadows began to lighten by some mysterious accord. Once again every molecule felt like it was shifting. No decision about coming or going came but a freedom around the question opened up. All the pressure I was putting on myself went away. The next day, January 2nd which was St. Therese's birthday, was the day of clarity. What preceded the answer was a willingness to go in either direction. Without thinking it consciously I had let go of attachment to either direction and this opened a fertile ground within me to hear or receive the answer. Like the days of old in Santa Cruz, I felt the top of my head open wide and sweetness poured in my like a waterfall. 'YES,' a clear yes to be Carmelite was all that I thought and felt.

This 'yes' created a force within me, and emotions of joy and peace replaced the worry and confusion. The latter never returned during all my days as Carmelite.

Feeling drunk in Spirit everyone else looked like they were part of the party too! At first I thought I was just projecting my happiness into the faces of everyone else but not long after my novice mistress said, 'Whatever is happening for you is affecting everyone else too. Sometimes this happens when a nun has a breakthrough,' she happily revealed.

My relationship with Sister Gemma changed at that point. Ease abounded. Our question time each morning in my cell became one of deep sharing about the writings of various mystics through the books she gave to me. I remember one time looking straight at her saying, 'One day you and I are going to found a monastery in the desert, and I think that I might also die in ten years.'

Where did that come from? I thought. There was nothing to back it up. We both thought we were here for the rest of our lives so it seemed ludicrous. The statements flew out of my mouth without much ado and were forgotten until about eight years later.

Our lives are an unfathomable mystery. We step into knowing occasionally but the entire scope would be impossible to comprehend. The best we can do say YES at each moment. Mother Anna pulled me aside a few days later, 'Sister Annunciata you need to make a decision, and if you are going to leave you need to do it now.' Her eyes laughed with a knowing glint. 'Ah, no, Mother Anna, I want to stay,' I laughed back realizing she was teasing me. Boldly she continued, 'You were in a trial of your vocation but it was so obvious all along you were meant to be Carmelite. No one could have told you, you had to find it out for yourself.' She sounded a little like the good witch Glinda in the *Wizard of Oz* when she told Dorothy that she could have gone home all along.

'Really? It was all so confusing' I admitted.

'She laughed a bit more, 'No, it was clear as day to all of us; we were just waiting.' I was shocked. It seemed to me with all my ugliness coming out they would be feeling the opposite about me being there.

Where to have me work during the day was a difficult process for both me and my superiors.

My first project took place in our windowless carpentry shop. I was asked to refinish the cabinet doors of part of the kitchen. Chuckling arose as I tried to recall if I ever did *anything* with wood before. Despite the dark windowless carpentry room the project was interesting. Sister Rita was assigned to show me what to do. This nun was about twenty years older than me yet looked radiantly young. She managed the kitchen, the farming, the milking of the cows and was adept in the very skills needed to keep a big self contained community sustainable. Sister Rita was a true anchor in the community. Silently she demonstrated each step attentively. First she showed me how to scrape the old varnish with random scraps of glass, then how to sand, re-stain, re-varnish and finally replace each door.

My fingers soon became very sensitive to how different thicknesses of glass would peel away the varnish. Thick shards void of narrowed angled edges were useless. The surface would glaze over the door leaving a light cloudy line with the old finish still intact. Ultra thin shards didn't work well either. They would either break or dig unevenly under my clumsy fingers. Not long into the project I figured out quarter inch think, triangular pieces with a gradual angle on the edge used to scrape worked perfectly. What was really cool were the unexpected moments when everything worked in unison to produce a long varnish peeling? This masterpiece would resemble a long uninterrupted string of apple skin.

Day after day I descended. My steps would take me from the light filled white colored corridors down the back stairwell to the dark, damp, unpainted concrete walls and floor of the basement.

This isolated job left me alone with my thoughts. It was my uninterrupted initiation into the distracted workings of my mind. Even if pre-monastery life was filled with times of solitude, it was always punctuated with jobs and school and friends. All of these were a veil hiding the continual stream of thoughts and feelings. Now this veil was pulled back to reveal a naked mind and heart in all their compulsions and restlessness.

The first wave of being unable to quiet my mind evoked agitation. I was annoyed with myself, 'Here you finally have time, endless time, to commune with God and you're wasting it,' the judge within me would rant. Under the conditioning of society I tried to manhandle my mind into stillness. I tackled it into a full body wrestle and the mind pulled out its strength rising up in resistant defiance. Oftentimes my mind would call upon emotion to back it up in its reticence to let go of its opinions and recollections.

Quickly this mind of mine taught me that *it will not be forced.*

My attempt to force seemed to be an approach in my mind's home territory giving me the disadvantage. My thoughts even turned my very desire for dwelling in the presence of God into a superficial dialogue keeping me away from stillness.

The doors were done in about a month; and the crash course of gentle observation of the mind had been strengthened within.

At this point I was put into a job that my leaders hoped would be long term. Office work was the financial mainstay for our community. Even though we lived frugally and grew most of what we ate, there were inherently large costs for sustaining a twenty person community. We were fortunate to have generous donations from those who we called friends so our role of writing letters of support to them was integral to our lives. Our letters were not only thank you notes; they were also our form of spiritual companionship. I was excited at the prospect of voicing words of consolation and gratitude, but found quickly I was unable to fit the protocol required. My first letters were rejected. The novice mistress patiently showed me the intricate system of answering mail. It was a masterpiece of detailed design. When a letter came to us we would pull the hand typed index card with their information. Computers were just coming on the social scene so all our correspondence was done with traditional old time manual typewriters. The name and address were typed with each line indented one or two spaces, creating a tiered reference. There were specific places on this 3"by5" card where all past correspondence, pertinent life facts and any prayer requests were recorded in abbreviated code. While I fumbled with the level of detail it would have been manageable over time. My real failing was the letter writing itself. The language we used was extremely flowery. We were also expected to follow a very specific format for what was said and how it was expressed. It felt like a form letter but was not treated like one. We were supposed to 'feel' the method as though it was our own style of writing which I wasn't able to do honestly.

With my failing in the office I was perceived as 'not being as smart as they thought I would be,' as one superior mentioned, which didn't hurt my feelings at all. At the same time I hungered for some kind of stimulation, something that would challenge my mind to stretch and learn. Instead of reaching out for traditional ways this would happen, I decided to focus on growing in wisdom. This way everything around me became a stimulating learning opportunity.

After the short stint in the office I was given another project in the basement. My novice mistress led me down the long, cold, clammy corridor of the cellar to a door at the end of the hall. Musty air billowed towards us as the door was pulled back like it had being waiting to be released for years. Wondrous to the eyes however was an old printing press with all the metal type heaped in dust laden drawers. It looked incredibly valuable. 'We need all the type sorted and cleaned,' stated the novice mistress,' someone is coming to buy it from us.' At first I rose to the new challenge but this excitement lasted maybe a few days. The tediousness of the job coupled with the stark working environment quickly tested my zeal. At least a small two foot by two foot window let in a little light. This learning was to tap into how I could embrace the work in new ways. It was a learning to get in touch with emotions that would be honest. Sometimes zeal was what I could harness. But when zeal was unavailable I tapped endurance. If endurance felt too hard acceptance was always a willing consort, and so on. There seemed to be no end to all these tiny letters. It was impossible to clean them in groups because the dust was caked into the small metal grooves. My greatest inner quality seemed to be playfulness. Sometimes I would laugh my way downstairs, 'here I go to prison for a few hours,' acting the part for the fun of it.

This too shall pass. And it did.

CHAPTER FOUR

A Banquet Set

Swells of luminous rainbow like arches lift my feet into the air
brushing the tips of grassy blades swaying in the wind of the spirited surge

like a dance of heaven and earth.

Life urges. Life surges.
And I ride the wave...
Dense. Subtle.
Indescribably bursting with a cacophonous utterance
    pushed and pulled from the fiber of my being,
        the fibers of created.

You. You are my life. I am this life. We are.

Who else can I possibly thank?
There is only you,
        always you.

Thank you.

THE DARK BASEMENT JOB was completed soon enough. With it an era was ended ushering in a new era of playful light jobs.

It was a funny turn of events that turned things around. Once a year the novices would cook dinner (the main meal at noon) and supper (the night meal at 6pm,) for the community. You could liken the day to a sorority game. It became more of a joke than a genuine relief for the main cooks. The day was the feast of St. Martha, who cooked the meal in Lazarus' house for Jesus and probably started as a custom giving the novices a chance to imitate Martha. Stories abounded about burnt hamburgers, raw spaghetti and veggies cooked into mush being served up on the day. It was our turn. The three of us novices sat in our classroom to decide the menu, free of any expectations of us other than poorly tasting half cooked concoctions. We sat there and neither Sister Perpetua nor Sister Teresita said a word. Inside my head ideas were popping like popcorn but I kept silence since I was the youngest. I thought we would all be bursting at the seams with the rarely given license for creativity.

Finally it seemed my ideas might help to fill the empty paper sitting before us awaiting a menu. The words blurted out of their own accord. 'What about spinach crepes with a hollandaise sauce, salmon pate and sherry mushroom soup, and….' Dinner and Supper were all expressed in one breath. Shock followed. My shock really. Sisters Teresita and Perpetua loved every idea. My worry of being too dominant was allevi-ated. The menu was approved instantly probably tongue in cheek by the sub-prioress whose refined taste was somewhat feared in the community. I remember her saying once to me, 'meat should always be cooked well done in our community, women prefer well done,' as though a general statement about all women for all time could be made. The fact that I loved medium rare from a young age was not a comment I preferred to make as you can imagine.

We were in the flow that day. The pressure of getting it all done in an hour dangled without influence in the magic of creativity. Grins ran across our three faces as we pulled back the cover on our creations in the hope to please the stomachs of our sisters. Just as sorority leaders might do, the leaders remained reserved, even poker faced as they dished up.

The three of us huddled in the kitchen with sheer glee, jumping up and down, 'We did it! We actually did it!' The night meal was equally delicious and our leaders were warmed by our innocent excitement, commenting out loud on one flavor or another. At the end of the meal we gathered for a movie and Mother Anna looked straight at me with all the other sisters gathered around, 'Sister Annunciata, we had no idea...' her voice trailed. 'What is she talking about?' I pondered quizzically. Embarrassment rose in red fleshed tones from my gut into my face. She was giving *me* credit for the meal even though we all cooked it together.

The next day the novice mistress led me to the kitchen. I stayed there for the rest of my days in North Dakota. These were the happiest of days.

The kitchen was a large corner room with windows spanning two of the walls and bright sunlight flood every counter. It felt like a sunny porch framed by the many shades of green foliage outside waving to us in the wind. 'Hello! Hello!' the leaves seemed to shout. They seemed to herald the end of my trial working in the dark corners of the basement. Since we grew most of what we ate cooking, canning and preserving was an ongoing daily task. The textures of freshly picked fruits and vegetables ran under our fingers, the rainbow of colors, and the overlapping aromas made each work shift a mini-banquet. Sister Elijah, the December 6th Santa Claus, became my co-worker and conspirator while Sister Rita shared her genius by teaching us all she knew from growing up on a farm not far away. She was the kitchen manager and only showed up to teach when needed.

I was really not sure what Sister Elijah thought of me but I absolutely loved her. Once we learned how to work in silence together playfulness was our daily lot. Over time we were called kitchen renegades. We took the community by storm as our ability to co-create grew. The way was paved by first learning how to communicate in silence. We were given permission to write notes even though I was only a novice. In the beginning I was so slow and bumbling. Sister Elijah had to carry the bulk of the meal just for us to finish on time. We only had an hour and fifteen minutes to cook everything from scratch for an entire community of twenty along with special foods for our chaplain and caretaker. A pile of scrap paper would sit out with pencils close by as we scrawled quick pressured questions hardly discernible. Just like learning the chant, cooking dinner in such a short amount of time was a real learning process. But once again it happened. My thoughts and motion became streamlined, giving me the clear insight *that we are capable of much more than we think, if only we step into the possibility.*

At first she would compose the menu and assign me a task or two. She kept the harder parts for herself like soufflés, sauces and casseroles. Once she saw me pick up speed the menu would lay open for us to each choose what we wanted to make. And not long after that we started adding in extra jobs like churning butter and baking bread pudding or cooked apples for other meals. All our preparation happened with a small traditional oven and four burners. Oftentimes we stacked pots to double cook. When we left for prayer everyone would go into the oven like an impressive gymnastics feat of balance and coordination.

One of my first stir fries is quite memorable. All was prepared with ease with just a little more stirring to mix in the cornstarch. This stir fry I was using an ancient spatula to stir. Its wooden handle had seen many years and the rubber head was mildly cracked. It was our old dependable capable of stirring any large amount of food with ease. Setting the spatula in the mixture for just a moment I turned my hand to the rice. Moments later grabbing the spatula handle I could see that part of it had broken off into the mix! Alarm ran through me as I pictured someone in my community getting the piece in their food. The rubber was the exact color of the noodles and my search for it was in vain. Notes scribbled back and forth between us. It was time for Sext and we had to leave. Sr. Elijah assured me she would find it when she returned to set the food out.

So, I trusted. Well, I trusted a little. As each line of a psalm chanted through my lips my thoughts posed questions in equal rhythm, 'Would she find it? What was going to happen? Why couldn't I help?' After Sext we would kneel in silence for seven minutes for a midday examination of conscience. During this time I thought about how I wanted to get out of there and help look for the piece of spatula cooking in my stir fry.

It was my duty to help serve the food that week which gave me permission to leave earlier than the other nuns. Once the time came I brushed the kneeler with a kiss and raced to the kitchen, 'Did you find it?' I anxiously wrote to her on a note. 'No, but it is okay. I sifted the entire stir fry. It must be dissolved, no one will choke or even notice,' she attempted to reassure me. This was not good enough. Without her seeing I wrote a note on a piece of scrap paper and plopped it on the serving table in front of the pot, 'BE CAREFUL!' it said in caps, 'PIECE OF SPATULA LOST IN STIR FRY!'

The leaders were shocked to see the note, I am not sure if it was the message or the audacity of putting a note, but they jolted a look in my direction. I shrugged my shoulders then dropped to the floor and kissed it to acknowledge the mistake. No one said anything to me after that, and we never learned what happened or who ate it. This was perhaps the hardest part of living in community; others had to suffer your own shortcomings. It was also the most tangible experience of unconditional love. The message came every day we were accepted not in spite, but in light, of who we were.

Stir fries seem to have a theme. Another was planned down the road and once again was on my list for the meal. Half way through the preparation I realized that I had forgotten to take the turkey out of the freezer! It would never thaw in enough time to put in the pot. Sr. Elijah, again the patient assuring friend, put the meat on the radiator. We kept an eye on its painfully slow progress in thawing. About 10 minutes before we would need to leave for prayer it was certain that it would not thaw in enough time. 'Don't worry, it will thaw in time,' she assured. But instead

I grabbed the meat deciding to let the prioress know my mistake by running down to her office. It was incredibly silly and Sister Elijah opposed me. To my surprise she grabbed the other end of the Ziploc bag and tried to pull the meat out of my hands giving me a look, 'OOOOOOH no you don't!'

'Ooooh yes I do!' and I pulled the bag towards me. Looking straight at each other we began a tug of war over the meat.

At one point her hands slipped and I raced with the meat towards the door but she caught me and our fight landed us right in the hallway. Our eyes were laughing while our hands were grasping with determination and our lips were set. Who would have known we had it in us?! Eventually her hands slipped again and she threw them up in exasperation. Closer and closer we grew like two peas in a pod.

Monastery life created this light way of sharing funny things that would happen in the day. At recreation we would hear about sheets getting tangled in the snow, flowers blooming in strange ways, the dog doing his funny butt dance in front of the crucifix shrine, and on it went. It seemed we touched the essence of who we were. In October we had one such recreation.

It was a magnanimous autumn evening with a full moon. We called them harvest moons and this one was the largest I had ever seen, dangling its deep orange hues so low to the horizon it tempted us to wonder if the plump ball would plop upon the plains with the slightest of breezes. We bolted energetically out the back door plunging into the evening sky. Greeting us was a large flat bed trailer overflowing with corn shucks donated from a local farm, and a large 10 foot by 10 foot cardboard box with a bottom but no top. We had just received our yearly supply of stuffing for our home sewn mattress tickings. Somehow we had to store all these shucks in our basement, and this evening I learned how.

Flipping on our gardening gloves the sisters swooped large armfuls of shucks from the trailer to the box. Without hesitation I joined the party and within minutes we had filled the box to overflowing. Needing to pack them I offered to jump inside and stomp the shucks. The Novice Mistress readily consented. As soon as I started jumping Sister Perpetua and Sister Teresita joined me. It was like we were on a trampoline laughing and knocking into each other. Actually it felt a more like we were in a giant playpen playing in the vast creation. I could not have imagined a better pastime. Spending an evening under this harvest moon, in the green oasis we called a back yard, playing in this life size pen with my sisters was sheer joy.

They were all my mentors, all of them and each of them. And I was it clear as the harvest moon dominating the horizon they bore me Christ. A word, a gesture, everything spoke to me, and they were words of blessing. More than blessing really, more like a hand reaching into my heart and caressing it from the inside out. They were my teachers: the sisters, the flowers, the chant, the silence, and the moon, all of them Christ. This continual bearing created bonds of trust and surrender from me to Him whom I had chosen for my own. The lessons of love were gentle, taking me to places deeper than the earth and higher than the sky. In flight I could say with John of the Cross that I forgot all but the Light, welcoming the loss to find myself no longer tethered.

The shucks were stored away in the cellar until early January. Sister Perpetua and I were told to fill a ticking with corn shucks and bring it into a newly prepared cell in our Novitiate. Why? Because a new woman was going to join us! The task was easy except that we had to figure out what to do in silence without any notes. Sister Perpetua was a great leader so I followed her direction. The mattresses themselves were a work of genius. One sister would sew a piece of material into a large bed size pillow we called a ticking. On one side would be an open slit about 3 feet long that could be semi-closed with a few small snaps. The material would be filled with corn shucks until it looked like a huge cylinder. Then the mattress would be placed upon one or two long boards set upon two low saw horses. Charmingly simple the cylinder would sit so high upon its frame we would have to climb up to get into bed. This lasted about a week until the body weight pact the shucks, releasing the air. Sister Perpetua and I stuffed and stuffed and stuffed. She motioned to push towards the ends as hard as we could, then we stuffed even more. There came a point no more shucks could possibly enter the mouth of the ticking. We swept the layer of dust from the floor and proceeded to move the whale like mattress. We could not even get our arms around it to lock fingers. I picked up the front and Sister Perpetua picked up the back and then, the comedy began.

Waddling with our creation through the basement hall bumping the walls on either side produced a series of small giggles. First the giggles came from me, then her, then me and then her. The basement door was too small for our whale to fit so had to shove it through the door jam. With me laying halfway on the steps pulling and Sister Perpetua using all her body weight on the pushing end the mattress finally burst into the stairwell. We flew to the floor in the wake of its movement. Giggling continued but we were able to maintain custody of the eyes which helped keep everything. The cumbersome bundle had to be pushed up the stairs, around the 180 degree turn in the stairwell, and through two more doors. Getting it to the top doorway was easy. The next door required more pushing and pulling, scattering shucks and laughter in every direction. Giggles were impossible at this point. Our laughter burst forth in waves as we fell with our whale through the next doorway. By this time we had caught each other's eyes, both brimming with joyful tears causing our laughter to magnify. Her bright red cheeks were enough to tickle me infectiously as we rolled against the walls opposite each other. Here we sat. 'Aaaaahhhhh,' we both eventually sighed.

The mattress took its rest on the wooden bed frame next to my cell. Only one week later our new entrance took place. The day was January 23rd, the feast of the espousal of Joseph and Mary. This time I could be part of the sisterly excitement instead of being the one received. Just like last year for me the grille remained open after communion and the Prioress and Novice Mistress stood inside awaiting the words of the short ritual.

We all watched her as she walked to the threshold. She was much quieter and serious than I had been. But then again, anyone would have been less demonstrative than me.

Our new sister was very reflective, shy yet perceptive. I was the lucky one to show here around like a big sister. Pride for our lifestyle never showed itself as strong as in this orientation. Her presence brought it forth from wells I had not known existed. My duty of cleaning the chapel passed on to her, as was our tradition. It seemed I had just been given the duty when the time came to give it away. The large swivel headed dust mop surrendered itself into her hands and I ran through the tasks in the order they were given to me. I reflected back to the time when Sister Teresita was cleaning the chapel until I took it over. This was only last year. My holy hour was during her cleaning time. It surprised me how enjoyable it was to have her there. Even though we might like our private time to be private I felt the opposite. As Sister Teresita swept the floor with the large swivel head mop her recollection and rhythm would intensify my own stillness.

The other duty to change hands was the bouquet preparation for choir. There were two statues, Joseph and Mary, set in alcoves on either side of the large grille. Fresh flowers were kept here for most of the year. Since they framed the sanctuary the bouquets were visually important. My arrangements were usually dismal. Once in a while would I create a bouquet that looked beautiful but those times were rare. We were given twenty minutes each day for the task. This meant we needed to choose vases, run out to the gardens and clip flowers, then prepare them inside. How could anyone human accomplish this? I tried and tried and never got the hang of it. My bouquets generally looked disheveled. Eventually I resorted to filling vases with water then running out the back door with the vases and clippers both in hand. Rushing through the yard I would clip the flowers and plop them into arrangements on the fly. At least my tactic kept me on time. The flowers would sprawl in the vase like they had just been uprooted from their favorite resting place and were upset to be in this new home.

However our new sister, eventually Sister Ruth created arrangements that took your breath away.

My thoughts evolved in direct relation to my letting go personal limitations. An interesting part of the dance was to understand that little things matter and do not matter all at the same time. Life is both serious and not serious at the same time.

Many occupations perhaps like a driven corporate career the focus stays frequently on the end goal without equal focus on balance along the way. Life here was all about navigating everything with that balance. This balance creates a mingling of serious and not so serious. Think about it. In one sense our spiritual growth is the most important thing in the world. And in another sense we can hardly take ourselves seriously in an area so far beyond our understanding.

One way I learned about this is in relation to my angels. They seemed to never hear my important prayers. There would not be signs or help in what I felt were my most confusing moments in religious life. It would seem they had left me. Then in all the really little things like getting to choir on time, they would show up like Johnny on the spot. I remember one time on the back porch there was a whispering in my ear, 'Benediction....benediction.... it is time,' the sound came in an etheric tone impossible to put into words, the utterance felt like shafts of light. Their point was that I was late. I had forgotten we were starting Vespers early so we could have Exposition of the Eucharist and Benediction! This was all fine and good, even playful. When I asked them to help me with some inner dilemma however, they were nowhere to be found. What is up with that? It was a lesson to me that the way we seek is the way we find. When I came from a place of desperation the very quality of my search for an answer limited the ability to receive the answer. And when I came from a place of open free expectation the answer would show up immediately.

The angels really did come to my aid many times. Every other day the cows would be milked and about ten two liter jugs would arrive to the back door. Sister Perpetua and I were called to bring the glass containers to the kitchen. We bustled through the task by taking one two liter jug in each hand, relying upon the hold of our palms upon the lid and neck as we ran up the flight of stairs. Our novice mistress held the door for us at the top. The third trip up the stairs with Sister Perpetua a couple steps ahead of me I tripped. The moment my Birkenstock sandal caught the step there was no recovery. Everything moved into slow motion as the jugs and I splattered upon the steps. I could feel were angels holding me as I fell, face first, on the steps. The jugs crashed on either side of me exploding into shards of glass and milk. As quickly as it happened it was over, and I laid there with glass all around me. Sister Perpetua and Sister Gemma were terrified. I knew nothing all was well having felt the angels hold me but all they could see was me lying in a sea of broken glass and blood. I was told not to move an inch. Slowly, ever so slowly, they cleaned each step until I could be reached and lifted. Copious blood was coming from my wrist the only place gashed by a piece of glass. 'You are protected by angels! My novice mistress exclaimed, 'Thank God we will not lose you.' Full of emotion she saw it as a sign.

At some point I began to have a hard time turning the tabernacle light off. We rotated the task and one sister would have the duty for a week before it passed to the next sister. For a good year and a half the job was easy but then I began to forget. Not just occasionally but almost always. At first it was easy to go with the flow of my mistake. But as I tried harder to remember and continued to fail the mistake began to absorb my focus. Since it was my duty for a week, I decided to embrace it like a challenge. It became a playground to accept myself without judgment and to also find a new way to remember. Nothing seemed to work. It sounds trivial but this was not just once a day, but at least eight to ten times a day for prayer *and* Mass!

As we would leave choir I would focus all my attention on remembering the light. Then a slight jostle of the door by the sister ahead of me, or the cat running by, would take my attention and the light remained on.

If it was left on you were buzzed to the office to be told to turn it off. 'Buzzzzz, Buzzzzz, Buzzzz, buzz-buzz,' would ring through the halls after Terce, after Sext, after None and on it would go.

'Ugggghhhh, again, I did it again,' and I would race from the other side of the monastery, stop at the prioress' office, then run to turn it off. All the sisters had to put up with that buzz.

To try to remember I made up a little jingle to sing on my way out to help. Failed. I tried notes of various sizes and colors. Once we finished prayer I held the note before my eyes as we left. Failed. Everything I tried failed and my resilience turned to discouragement. One evening after a day of forgetting the tabernacle I knelt for the time of meditation and my heart sank. It sank just like it did in the story about the coke glasses when I was seven. At that moment I opened the Bible asking Jesus to help me. The passage where he was walking on the water lit up like a light bulb. Stifling tears I read the passage as the words warmed my heart. Peter had just asked Jesus if it was truly him walking on the water to call him (Peter) to walk on the water to as well to meet him (Jesus.) As Peter stepped onto the water he excitedly began walking like Jesus. The wind picked up and when he felt it he doubted and began to sink. As he sank the passage continued, '*Immediately*, Jesus reached out his hand and saved him.' The word immediately felt like a hand reaching into my discouraged heart and lifted me up. The feelings disappeared in that moment; and what was even more amazing was my difficulty in remembering the tabernacle light disappeared entirely as well.

The tabernacle light let me increase trust, trust in the face of my own mistakes. Trust is a quality of soul that brings us to greatness, not a greatness accord to society's standards, but one that stands free to act and love in the face of whatever happens in life.

The rhythm of life in North Dakota was the epitome of consistency. Everyone had their responsibilities all the way down to who opened the shades on which windows during the five minutes between Morning

Prayer (Lauds) and the hour of meditation; and the times of chant and meditation happened as faithfully as sunrise and sunset.

Silence was the blanket joining us close to the Beloved. Silence set no limits upon how much we snuggled, kissed, made love, or in our dark moments, withdrew. Every nun kept the secrets of the King in her solitude. Wrapped securely thus the shadow would not persist for long before the eyes of the Beloved would pierce and dissolve the division drawing us close. It is a faithfulness of Spirit to always desire, always seek, always find and always succeed in reaching its creation.

The second Lent was my first year of repeating ritual. There was a certain satisfaction in coming full circle, a feeling of 'having arrived.' Lent raced into Holy Week and soon the Last Supper was upon us. This was the very celebration where I experienced Christ dramatically the first year. The Triduum was no less spectacular in fact it was more breathtaking. The rituals kept opening up wider and wider as our ability to receive grew. Repetition was not mundane. This second year my fingers moved nimbly through the many pages and books, my voice rose easily with the vaguely familiar rhythm of the Lenten tones, and my heart was freed from concentrating upon following everyone. 'This is how they h feel,' I thought of the nuns. Now I could offer Sister Ruth the understanding given to me. Her tension was palpable as she pulled one book, then another, from her shelf. She raced through pages to the one my finger gently and knowingly indicated, just like Sister Perpetua had done for me. As Lent exploded into Easter, and Easter held its seven week wake of liturgical feasts, summer came upon us...

SECTION THREE

New Life

Page after page
I turn the page of you
reading on with measured ravenousness
your Being unraveling and unfolding
simultaneously, laying bare
with non-reflecting confidence

Clear we are, fresh and clean
like newly washed, crisp, white sheets
flapping in the wind and sun

Security lingers, weighting words
sinking them deep in the heart
where they root themselves
proud to populate the land

You take me aloft
willing I go with You far, far away

Our eyes sparkle with the light of a blue-gold horizon

CHAPTER ONE

A Bride of God

My words fall like a gentle rain
*   or a ray of sunshine*
Moving swiftly and vastly
*   nourishing without force*
*   enlivening unnoticed*

Words dance with words
tingling the spine of creation
up and down, up and down
*   until they swell into something never heard before*

Ever new, yet ever ancient
An eternal word is my word, your word
And all is owned yet all is gift.

SUMMER CAME UPON US but not before I was invited to take simple vows. By this point there was no question in either the community's mind or my mind about my calling or whether I fit in community. The grace of January 2nd created a solid foundation for us to be one family.

'Can you make a list of people you want to invite?' Mother Anna asked, and the next day she received a piece of paper with over two hundred names.

'Why? Why would you invite so many people?' she probed, to which the natural response came, 'Why wouldn't we tell all my family and friends? It is one of the most important days of my life!' Since the tradition was to allow the woman to choose how many she wished to send they did not try to dissuade me. And since this was my one and only window to communicate with all the people I loved my mind cast the widest net possible, reaching into caverns of memories for names. Into each envelope an announcement, a homemade silk screen holy card with an inspirational quote for the profession day, and copious silent heart-felt intentions were sealed and mailed.

The ritual ceremony for the simple vows was a version of the early consecration of virgins in the Christian communities. The service looked enamoring, using language of marriage between God and the soul, the title, however, jolted me. The program was titled <u>Solemn Consecration of Virgins</u>. 'I'm not a virgin,' I worried, 'Am I allowed to take these vows?'

Troubled, my thoughts persisted, 'I had no idea we had to be a virgin to be a Carmelite, what am I going to do? Is everyone here a virgin? Wouldn't that be a question they would ask before you entered?' Dragging my feet I asked to see the Novice Mistress and the Prioress to tell them the truth. Thinking this could be the end of my stay my voice quivered, 'I…..I….I'm not a virgin,' finally blurting it out, and with it my surrender to the consequences. 'And the words of the ceremony refer to me as a virgin,' my mouth uttered assuming they did not know.

They started laughing. 'Of course we knew you were not a virgin,' they both responded. 'It's just a symbolic service representing spiritual virginity.' I wondered how they knew but the question faded quickly in relevance. 'This was actually going to happen; I was actually going to be a Carmelite!'

This moment was not the only time of love undoing all. This love had come to me before in my first soul mate in my senior year of high school. It was all consuming as well. But this love between us was for a time and not a life time. Circumstances created an inability to find each other as he entered the Air Force and I moved. We were in a society still absent of cell phones and internet and it seemed the hand of Providence was taking us on different paths. In the face of this great loss discernment came to me to give wind beneath my wings. Discernment by my definition is the freedom to understand, act and/or choose the option of highest good in any situation. And blessed are we when our very discernment gives us joy! So it was in relation to my soul mate, there was joy in accepting that our being together was not meant to be because it was for our highest good.

Very little preparation was needed to get ready for the ceremony. Even though the script for the ritual was intricate, most the words were for the presiding priest and most the chant was for the community of nuns. I had two chant responses and otherwise was on the receiving end of every consecrating prayer. Father Bernard was coming to officiate! Along with my family coming, this was the greatest gift of all. Mother Anna called me to her office one day, 'I want to show you your wedding gown,' she happily pulled a box off the side table. 'So we do not get to choose our own gown and have it sent to us?' I blurted with a bit of surprise, though not sure why I would think they would give that option. 'Oh no, we have one that every sister wears, along with the shoes and stockings,' she responded, overlooking the tinge of sadness in my question. The dress looked like something a shy woman would wear in the 1950s. The material was thick and A-framed with long sleeves ending in ruffles. A similar ruffle ran across the chest with one last smaller ruffle at the top of the high neck, landing just under the chin. The shoes went perfectly with the dress, sad to say. They looked like old nursing shoes with thick buckles. The thick, white, knee high stockings must have been made for circulation given how tightly they gripped the leg. In the end it did not matter to me, after all was I not going to have to see myself but it would all come off half way through the ceremony to be replaced by my Carmelite Habit.

You have to love synchronicity. The very date of my simple vows was July 15, 1992. July 15th was the same day that my soul mate and I chose to make love for the first time years prior and once my solemn vows would come around it would mark 10 years exactly. Here on the very same date a love consecration would take place building on love up to this point.

One week before the ceremony every sister makes a private retreat. You would think living in silence no retreat would be necessary but we all sink into habits and patterns that could use renewal, even in the silence. It was very exciting. I was given a very large black veil and a book that would be my guided retreat. All my meals would be taken in private. The veil would be worn as a symbol of the preparation taking place in my soul. The community focused on acts of special kindness. The door would be opened, my food tray would be set up carefully, and even flowers appeared near my silverware. There would come a day when I would be able to do the same for Sister Ruth.

The retreat surprised me; it was not a time of ease. I longed to be in community instead of more withdrawn.

The book I had been given felt superficial, it was hard to back pedal to first considerations of being a Bride of Christ when this was the primary reason I entered and was now years in its evolving. Resorting to a theology book in my room I took a chance and wrote a note to my novice mistress, 'Could you get me a book that would nurture my spirituality? This one I was given doesn't work at all.' The next day I found a thick book entitled, 'Retreat with John of the Cross,' my heart soared, 'something interesting!' Every day my eyes devoured the theme. His every word seemed filled with light and I found myself putting quotes on scrap papers in my prayer books, quotes that would stay with me all my religious days. Some of it felt a bit austere but you could feel his love for God and his willingness to be an empty vessel, he embodied what I longed to be which gave great ease in overlooking the older style language and austerity. Even with this great gift I couldn't wait for the retreat to be over. I missed recreation, I missed being in the kitchen, I missed all the ways we communicated without words to each other, now limited by the stupid veil that made it hard to see anything. Worse than all, the retreat felt barren, void of God's Presence, up until the last day. Waking that last day of retreat, July 15th, sweetness awoke me in the morning and carried me through the day. Wouldn't you know the very day consolation arrived would be the day interrupted with fittings and details.

The dress was easily tailored to my one hundred and ten pound body lean from the ever moving lifestyle and healthy farm produced meals. It was designed to fit anyone with a few tucks and releases. With the dress fitted, and the sewing room sisters buzzing around me with big smiles, I was grateful NOT to have a mirror. It saved me any discomfort of what I looked like for my wedding in that wedding dress.

The novice mistress was my companion for the day, and once the sewing was done she rolled my hair. We laughed and chatted about spiritual things, our only difference being her love of penance. In my mind it could all be driven by ego, I preferred to do what inspired more love within the heart. Nonetheless, we were becoming fast friends. She shared her perspective with warm openness.

In a funny turn of events an enduring misunderstanding happened for Sister Gemma and me. At some point in North Dakota she noticed I never ate peaches. It was true. They repulsed me. The slippery texture, the occasional rough edge from part of the seed, the corn syrup sauce all turned my stomach. She assumed I secretly loved peaches. For one of my feast days she procured peach preserves, peach cobbler, peach ice cream and cooked peaches to surprise me with enjoyment! Seeing her excitement led me to eat all of it without reserve. A few weeks later I thanked her profusely and let her know my real reason for not eating peaches. She did not believe me. Peaches became my reminder: love is in the intention and not in the gift.

Novitiate life continued to soften its edges as allowances were made for our desires. We began to pray charismatic style together. We sang charismatic songs from Steubenville. The novices introduced their own songs into big feast days, even Sister Perpetua were given permission to practice together on new harmonies. Sister Gemma went through a big breakthrough though she never shared it with us. In this she also lingered in my place of work seeking more of our inspiring conversation. I began to worry we were breaking silence. Feeling guilty and divided I took the concern to the confessional where the priest surprised me, 'Be happy to have such a friend,' he said, 'they do not come along often in monastic life.'

The day of preparation for my profession was no worry at all. Sister Gemma and I chatted like we were having a slumber party.

July 15th arrived and sunlight filtered into my cell as I lay upon the crunchy corn shucks below me. It was the only day where permission was given to sleep in or relax. Normally we jumped out of bed before dawn and prostrated on a cold floor in our tunics which suited me just fine. Contently resting my legs wriggled a bit to make new gulleys in the easily imprinted mattress. Corn shucks had no bounce. The weight of my body felt heavier than the mattress. Every bone and muscle sank into its own gully. Testing the mattress was the content of my morning, rolling a little to the left, a little to the right. 'Kkkysh, kkkysh, kkkysh,' sounded below me as the shucks rubbed against each other.

'Knock, knock, knock,' a light signal that it was time to dress. Sister Gemma entered my cell to help me. We both did our part in a silence that was not required. Some moments we sink deep where our breath is taken away and sometimes we rise high and our words become the fiery proclamation of the universe. Today it was the former. The rollers came out of my hair with locks bouncing down my back and shoulders. They felt thick and glamorous after two years of no haircuts.

My family had arrived during my retreat even though I had yet to see them. Their being there brought me back to so many memories of our journey together. Here was just another leg. Sometimes I have felt that

Mom, Dad, Kelly, Adam and I were together in the times of King Arthur sitting at the Round Table. Who knows, maybe one of us was King Arthur. It always felt our journey supported us in our personal mission.

Tight white stockings check. White nursing shoes with napkins stuffed into the toes so they would fit, check. White tunic freshly washed and pressed by my fellow novice Sister Teresita, check. White bridal gown zipped up the back, check. Hair pinned back and veil secured, check. We were ready to go. The first stop was to Mother Anna for approval.

'Uggggghhhhh,' she blatantly blurted out upon first seeing me, 'your hair looks terrible.'

Unaffected I laughed, 'Mother Anna, it's all going to be cut off in about an hour. Who cares?'

To which her eyes glimmered recognition. We had a great connection and she knew it. Somehow we both knew she could not get away with disapproval on this day that was *my* wedding day. We walked together to the chapter room. The solemn silence made the room pregnant with bridled excitement. We all stood there for a moment or two until the Prioress motioned it was time. One of the sisters rang a small bell whose sound unleashed the nervousness hidden deep in my gut. It was time.

The entire community began to chant. Two by two my sisters moved like priestesses into our choir where a large expectant group waited for us in the chapel. The hundreds of people present held a quiet that filled the air with sound.

The sisters all moved to their stalls while I continued by myself down the center of our wide choir, pacing myself to the words of the chant. The open grille revealed a kneeler decorated with satin and ribbons set in front of the altar. The chapel was filled with barely any standing room and all let out a soft 'ohhhhh' as I moved to my spot. Just to my right stood my parents, humbly standing side by side with looks of love and pride in their eyes.

Father Bernard had flown all the way out here to officiate an important moment in my life once again. Aware of my awkwardness to be in front of so many people, he would send winks sparking my own free spiritedness.

The sign of peace came before communion and the profession of vows. Mother Anna had told me I could reach out to my family. When the moment came I rushed to Mom and Dad telling them how much I loved them. We hugged long and strong, grabbing moments like they were our last. As I turned towards the chapel who stood in the front row but an entire slew of family and friends! My sister Kelly with her husband Stephen and two little girls Andrea and Monica, my little brother Adam, my Dad's siblings Betty, Gary and Sandy, spouses, my mom's Mom and Dad and even Cincinnati friends Maria and Jerry, Tom and Lisa. This gift was completely overwhelming. I rushed to hug them too.

As my family and I greeted each other joy rippled through the rows and attendees I did not know rushed towards me to hug and shake hands. Even though I was only instructed to give the sign of peace to my family, there was nothing I could do to stop the escalating movement other than greet them all like they were family. I felt like an ambassador of the Carmelites to these friends who knew us only through the sound of our chanting voices.

This lightened everything up and Father Bernard and I moved into the play we had always enjoyed. A series of questions requiring a YES from me and the community set the three year commitment in place. I was officially a bride of God and Christ. Now it was time to receive the Habit. Father Bernard motioned for me to come to the grille. He and I faced the people and the prioress and novice mistress stood in the choir just out of view.

The Prioress helped me unsnap the dress. Sister Gemma unpinned the veil. And I was left standing there in a thin white tunic. This was not all that was let go, Mother Maria Teresa motioned Father Bernard to the over sized scissors sitting on a stand decorated with an abundance of ribbons. He looked surprised. 'Me???' his glance went back and forth from her to me. I winked at him with a big smile and picked up the scissors myself plopping them in his hand. This friend of mine grabbed as much hair as his hands could hold and started to cut, or rather saw. The thick heavy metal rested on the nape of my neck as he slowly released the first clump. Mother Maria Teresa motioned to him to give this section to her. He started again as all the attendees made soft sighs. The hair would be given to my family as a surprise gift. My Dad would ultimately frame pieces of hair with programs from the ceremony and give them to all who had attended. I stood essentially unclothed before all who had ventured here today. I waited to be re-clothed in the consecrated garments of a Carmelite. Piece by piece was placed on my body as Father Bernard read the consecratory prayer that poetically revealed the symbolism.

The brown tunic, or 'Habit,' was an A frame garment reaching the floor. It came first zipping up the front and covering my arms with wide graceful sleeves reaching to my knuckles. Next was the toque, a white head covering tailored to fit the frame of my face. It covered half my forehead and sat just under my chin. The scapular was third. Its two panels, one laying down my front and one down my back looked like a narrow sandwich board sign. The Scapular was particular to the Carmelite Order. In the early 1200s a man named Simon Stock was the leader of the Carmelites during a time of great internal strife. In a moment of dismay this English man went to his private cell praying desperately to Mary for help. The Order was having struggles and he wondered if everything was going to fall apart and end. Mary appeared to him assuring him that she had a special love for this Order and that she would protect it. As a sign of her commitment she gave him a small piece of cloth with her image on it as a sign that would endure. After the vision the Order gained stability as she had promised. In the long run the Scapular became a miraculous object through which the person wearing it would experience miracles of healing. It became so popular throughout the world that the item took on its own cult separate from the Carmelites and was even used in first Saturday devotions and frequently part of the ritual preparation for children receiving their first Eucharist. I received one in second grade but never knew it was connected with the Carmelites, or even knew what a Carmelite was back then. Before the veil was placed a white plastic strip was put on top my forehead held on by elastic that stretched to the back part of my head. It created a bridge upon which the veil would sit and looked a bit like a priest's white collar.

Once clothed a small voice from the choir intoned the Te Deum, and I prostrated on a rug in the sanctuary just like priests do in their ordination. This ancient hymn celebrates angels, saints and all creation in God. Lying on the floor my spirit soared beyond boundaries as the unfolding of heaven on earth happened in this special moment.

Silence followed the exultant chant and my feet glided over the threshold.

The silence would segue into one large party inside and outside the monastery. I was guided to the speak room where streams of people flooded the doorway to take pictures and greet us. My Grandpa Wilson cried, Marcia grabbed me into a long bear hug and my sister held up Andrea and Monica so I could kiss them and hold them tightly. Sister Teresita had made a three tiered wedding cake with handmade flowers.

My dream was fulfilled. My dream was beginning.

Later in the day Mother Anna let me know I wasn't supposed to leave the sanctuary during the ceremony She said it violated canon law! We realized the misunderstanding soon afterward. She did not mean for me to give the sign of peace to my entire family she meant only my parents. The misunderstanding allowed a joyful occurrence that caused no harm.

A dream that week gave me deeper insight into this new level of consecration. The pope and I were standing talking intimately. He was dressed in white while I was completely naked. My skin glowed with brightness and not an ounce of self-consciousness existed. At one point the pope looked at me and said, 'Others need me to attend them now, but do not be afraid for I am with you and you will feel my presence in new ways. You do not need me in these ways anymore.'

His words sparked sadness at first. As his back turned towards me I felt the loss of something very familiar that was consoling, but simultaneously it felt like I was entering a different type of presence no less consoling. My vows were not just some kind of discipline or commitment; something was washed in me and taken into a more subtle level of being.

CHAPTER TWO
Simplicity Reigns

My soul, it sings a song
sounding through the airwaves of creation
coming from the Source unnamed
naming in celebration

The song sings me into Spirit's movement
The song lingers, lacing its tones in the grassy blades of existence
The song takes me on its ride of meaning unraveling

Spirit whispers in hush filled tones
I sing for you

DAYS ROLLED INTO WEEKS rolled into months. And the seasons over riding all our liturgical ones were those of nature. Living off the land created immediacy around having provisions. Just as we chanted a trust in God to take care of us, we worked with the land to see this care come forward with a cornucopia of fruits and vegetables. We lived in accord with the snow that would pile as high as our roof, and the winds that brought the snow. We lived in patient expectation as spring slowly melted the winter away and flowers bloomed again in our land. We spread manure and gathered seeds. We canned vegetables and picked our fruit fresh for the eating. Nature treated us gently, or perhaps we understood it for what it was. These seasons marked years for us, and each year showed us change. Even in a monastery change happens daily. Perhaps here, stripped of the layers of society, change could stand out even more.

To my happiness the roles of cooking our main meal and of taking out the compost continued throughout my time in North Dakota giving a solid structure to the ever deepening lessons of self and God. Food became a steady teacher. Potatoes were just one example. We ate them mashed, hashed, diced, chopped, layered, frittered, pancake style, and any other way we could concoct.

One popular way was pan fried chopped potatoes. Sister Elijah mastered these years back, now it was my turn. Mother Anna was specific in how they were prepared. Cutting them into half inch naked white cubes was easy. Heating the oil and adding the potatoes was of course, a piece of cake. The stress came when they needed to be turned. The first time I must have begun to turn the potatoes too soon. They were partially raw but I thought they would cook through. Six cups of potatoes needed to be fried in our skillet; some of them did not even touch the oil.

At the same time I was tending them, beets needed de-husking, carrots needed shredding and custard needed to get into the oven. The potatoes were looking pretty bad with some sides burning, others raw and some not getting to meet the oil at all. Sweat formed all over my body as I flipped them hoping for a miracle. They were turning into a disaster which meant the community was going to have to suffer for it. Sometimes the meals we provided were the major consolation they had after long fasts and many hours of hard work.

With the time for prayer upon us the potatoes went into the warm oven with the hope they would become edible in twenty five minutes. This would take the raw parts cooking and the burnt parts softening. I was asking for a miracle. Sext was a rigorous practice of turning my attention back to the present moment as it snapped like a rubber band to thoughts about the potatoes. Soon enough we were in the refectory for our meal. The serving sisters whisked the warming towels off the food revealing my potatoes half burnt, half raw. Since the youngest dished up last it was impossible for me to sift through the worse ones for myself.

After the meal and before the dishes I was called into Mother Anna's office. "I knew it," inwardly getting ready to hear what I dreaded to hear.

'Sr. Annunciata, THOSE POTATOES!" and I dropped to my knees and kissed the floor. She focused very little upon the mistake after that telling me to get up. Immediately she began advising me on how to make them better. 'When you are making the potatoes,' she began, 'first you leave them in the frying pan until the bottoms have just become golden brown, do not flip or touch them until that point, usually about ten minutes,' her confident voice paused only briefly. 'Easy enough,' I thought. 'This was not what I had done but it made sense.'

After they brown on the bottom side, drop everything else you are doing and focus only on the potatoes,' she went on. A huge 'Bu-u-u-ut,' silently arose from my belly stifled before it reached my mouth.

'Start flipping the potatoes in a slow continuous motion.' Her long fingers, slightly bent through arthritis yet elegant even in their age, modeled the motion. 'Keep flipping and do not do anything else until they are golden then quickly remove them.'

My mind zoned at this point as it burst into loads of defensive arguments, 'How can you tell me to drop everything else and also expect us to produce a meal for over twenty sisters?! Have you ever worked in a kitchen like ours?!' Her instruction felt insensitive to how hard I try and how little time we have.

When she finished I thanked her by kissing her Scapular and left.

Kissing the leaders' Scapulars was our way of showing gratitude or receiving blessing.

The following week our menu came back approved with one addition: my name was written in bright red felt tip pen next to the chopped potatoes. Our menus were written in light pencil upon scrap paper, so the red tipped pen looked like she was shouting at me. 'She is not even giving me the chance to sign up for them freely!' my sensitive nature rebelled. As the defenses brimmed, the opportunity before me unveiled itself. 'These potatoes and my reaction are giving me an opportunity to learn,' I thought quite seriously. 'I can use the potatoes as my means to practice presence with myself.'

This second try started out well as they browned undisturbed by a spatula. Once the potatoes reached the described golden tone, the heat was on (literally) and I set aside the other two items in nervous hope there would be time to finish them before prayer. My hand began its solitary task of flipping. 'A-a-a-ah, how nice is this to do just one thing at a time,' the contemplative moment surprised me. The feeling lasted until the judge poked its head into my joy, 'How can you be expected to complete everything?!' Its power dominated. Then the joy poked back, 'This is what is asked put loving attention here.' The ability to be present overrode the judge. Mother Anna's instruction made it easier to let go of pressures. My eyes took in the shapes and colors of the tiny white cubes that were my charge. She gave me the greatest of gifts which I had not even imagined. Because of her instruction every time I cooked the potatoes I had direct permission to do just one task. Sweet presence was mine. The potatoes turned out okay. They were not fabulous but not bad either. You would think the story ended here but it did not.

Next week once again the menu came back approved with my name written in red felt tipped pen next to those silly potatoes. Resistance rose seeing the red ink. 'Hadn't I learned my lesson?' I said to Mother Anna in my imagination. 'Can't you give me a break?' Somehow the red ink made me feel like a spotlight was on me. Week after week, month after month she continued to put my name in red ink next to the potatoes and I wondered, 'When is this going to end? It feels so severe, so rigid.' The potatoes let me run through a full range of emotions including irritation, sadness, grasping and discouragement. At times I wanted the red pen to not be there as a sign that I had done a good job. That red pen chose a different lesson each week. Layers of responses opened up my inner desire for approval. I stood as the loving observer slowly crafting a new form of security, acceptance and allowance. Each week as the potatoes were assigned to me I would dip into contemplative moments of flipping them, and each week all that needed to be done was completed.

At some point I was finally able to let go. I already enjoyed the pleasure of cooking them, sinking into the motion of flipping them until golden brown. Now was the added pleasure of acceptance without reason or security. It was a prize beyond imagining when my resistance faded away. I accepted the red pen. Most of the pain came from assuming the red pen was a message of disapproval. This was only opinion in my mind which meant it could just as easily be untrue. The potatoes began to turn our beautifully golden each and every time. The red pen could not be saying the job was not done well, for the evidence was in the pudding, or in this case, the potatoes. Years later she would reveal her motive to me reducing me to tears to learn how needlessly hard I had been on myself.

Life continued this soft flexible expansion. The organic nature of community impressed itself upon me. In the transparency of silence we knew each other without words. When a nun had a breakthrough her entire face changed. Sometimes she would look like a different person in the newfound joy and ease. All of us would be affected by the change of another. If this was so for us, I knew it affected our world as well. I knew that if a light shined a little brighter the whole of creation would necessarily be affected. Letters thanking us for answered prayers let us witness *their* faith, not so much ours. In our own way we were catalysts and facilitators. At times someone will say to me, 'It is so good you left the monastery for now you can work with people and be of service to their growth.' But I do not believe this is objectively true. Presence is the greatest influence. When we make choices in alignment with our soul's purpose, we contribute the greatest good. My life now is neither more nor less effective in service. It is simply in alignment with my journey like being Carmelite was in its time.

Taking out the daily compost to the deep hole at the end of the raspberry patch was my afternoon duty. For about half the year it was a ten minute task of running out the back door across the half acre of land with two to four buckets in my hands and a spatula to scrape them clean. The other half of the year the same task would take more than half an hour. The longer jaunt was during winter. During the cold season snow and wind used the land like an open canvas and our private oasis became an ongoing art project changing shape and contour daily. Once snow season set in taking the compost became a winter cross country ski sport. The powder like white fluff would stack lightly three to four feet high requiring me to learn how to glide lightly and quickly or else sink into a self made hole. My first attempts met with comical failure. Falling to the right or the left my Habit would quickly crust in the below zero temperatures. Gingerly I rolled myself back to standing. The snow was like quicksand where a dance of balancing poles, ski and body could last brief seconds before creating another hole. Learning to glide was survival at first, but adeptness ensued and the cold season became a winter wonderland. Sometimes the night winds would form drifts rising ten feet in shapes of waves. Heavier storms would leave trees bowing to my passing and I would bow back in reverence to them. The cemetery was en route and the statue of Our Lady of Mount Carmel holding baby Jesus would change attire frequently. One day the snow would form berets like the French, other days sombreros would be donned and still other times they bundled up like Eskimos. She was my Lady of all lands.

Seeing her would inspire snow angels once I knew getting back up was within my skills. 'Swish, swish, swish, my arms and legs would move back and forth,' strategically placing each angel behind her in a semi-circle. Only once was my extracurricular play found out when we all went for a winter hike one night. 'What is this??' The novice mistress looked at me. My eyes went downcast and a word was never said.

Moments of absorption came and went, and I developed an ability to welcome them in their coming and going. For many years they were my deep consolation but now my soul moved in and out of sensory moments with ease. It felt like a honeymoon phase had transitioned into true marriage where respect, depth and passion are cultivated in steady rhythm. Ecstatic moments still happened frequently enough to be part of my relationship with God. Most of the time it was unexpected like a Lover surprising his Beloved with flowers for no reason. In my cell for spiritual reading one morning the holy card marking my spot fell specifically into my hands. Jesus was tenderly holding a sheep as they were looking deeply at each other. The image felt alive as an image of Jesus and me! Time passed unnoticed and love flowed without any reservation. Directly we gazed at each other. Was it possible to have a Lover with greater tenderness than this God of mine?

Newly sewn multi-patterned colorful aprons awaited Sister Elijah and me one day in the kitchen. Bounding into the space at the usual ten o'clock time there they sat. About five or six different patterns cut in uniform pattern and neatly folded sat on the counter. We both chose our favorite patterns. Mine was brightly colored blues with green and orange swirls and Sister Elijah's was pink and white. They were shaped like a large tent. Tiny snaps placed on the seam of the upper back were the only means to keep the apron on. We had to snap them for each other each day as the snaps were just out of reach for backwards folded arms. The older solid colored aprons with traditional ties around the waist had been taken away. Giggling our way into the preparation Sister Elijah began chopping onions and I picked up the swiss chard to start the washing. Every once in a while we would look over at each other in these A framed aprons and start giggling again. With no forewarning Mother Maria Teresa and another sister briskly entered the kitchen. In her authoritative entrance she spoke freely. Whenever she was present silence or speaking was her option. So if she chose to start a discussion with everyone we could all talk as well. 'They are beautiful aren't they? One of our benefactors made them all for us,' she happily explained. I started laughing, 'Mother Maria Teresa,' sticking out my stomach as I responded,' I feel like Our Lady of Guadalupe.' Sister Elijah chuckled. 'Sister Annunciata,' Mother responded in a scandalized tone followed by an inevitable laugh.

My first year as a simple professed nun passed swiftly and the summer time ushered in my family visit. I couldn't wait to share with them about my first year in vows. I hardly slept as I imagined them in the guest room. Oddly the prioress told me to go in alone for a private visit. The leaders *always* joined us maybe the rules change once you are professed. My heart took a pause as my mom greeted me, sitting there alone. Somberness made the air seem gray and her face sat like stone. She looked so sad waiting for me. We sat for a few minutes awkwardly. Something was up but I had no idea what to say or ask. I sat down on the straight legged, hard wooden stool, mirroring the lack of comfort present in that moment.

Without small talk and heavy with hesitation she said it directly, 'Your Dad and I are getting a divorce.'

I was 27 years old. They had been married for 27 years. My family was my rock. Sadness poured upon me and welled up within me with a magnitude beyond what my mind could process. Sitting there was like sitting in the middle of nowhere. We didn't talk much as all the words drained out my feet leaving me there limply. My visit with my mom ended fairly quickly not because we didn't want to be together but only because the emotion left us both speechless. Mom shared a few of her reasons and how things were going but she hid most, sensitive to my own shock. It struck me how courageous she was in that moment.

My dad came in afterwards, 'I'm sorry Kim, I am so sorry,' choking words came from his throat as tears ran down his face. My tears followed. Our hearts shared a thousand words that our mouths did not need to express.

The rest of the visit became an awkward juggling of seeing them separately. These would be my only moments with them. Once they left I would not be able to call or visit and the separation my lifestyle imposed became just that, an imposition. Dad and I talked about my leaving as a real possibility. In the end he encouraged me to stay, 'We'll get through this together, let's just follow the rules for now and see how it all goes.' Mom hoped I would not leave just because of the divorce.

Food lost all flavor and night after night I cried myself to sleep. At one point I asked to see a counselor to help me move through the deep grief. She was not closed to the idea, but certainly did not encourage it. 'Spend time with Mother Anna and see if she can help you first,' Mother Maria Teresa suggested. The suggestion made it clear that outside support is our *last* resort. I never asked again though I suffered greatly without having someone with whom to talk. Mother Anna was kind but not quite the type of emotional support for which my heart longed. What did I need? To cry, to lament the loss, to talk about all the things I loved about my family, to have a friend walk with me in these sad moments. So I cried in my cell at night. Poor Sister Ruth whose cell sat next to me undoubtedly heard my copious sobs. She started showing me the greatest care and tenderness. Her gestures and expression said, 'I am with you, I am praying for you.' Silently a deep friendship emerged. As far as I knew the community was not told at first. In time my loss prompted Mother Maria Teresa to share with me the other sisters whose parents had divorced. Even she had lost both her parents in a car accident when she was very young. We walked like heroines providing space, care and understanding in the inevitable turns of life.

Our humanity was the means in which God spoke to us in community. It is humbling yet liberating to allow both our strengths and weaknesses to be the channel of Spirit. One evening my prioress made a small mistake which reminded me of this truth. All of us were recreating together, professed and novices, which happened only occasionally, and Mother Maria Teresa made a joke about me. She commented on how I only play really sad pieces of music on the organ. The arrow struck my heart. She realized with surprise what she had done as our eyes locked in a gaze. In that moment I saw her. In that moment her care showed itself not so much in words but in the meeting of souls. And I had no doubt the small mishap was a simple slip That evening during Compline the hurt of the statement came to me along with a passage from Scripture alighting in my heart. The words were a parable, 'you have been forgiven much, forgive her this small transgression,' and all hurt disappeared.

Loss is part of life. It is part of the rhythm of birthing, living, dying and re-birthing. Not long after my parents' visit there was another loss. Our older Sister Clementine passed away. Her impending death was clear to me for her sweet benign disposition turned cranky. Many times I had nursed men and women close to their time of passing. Standing beside them a full range of emotions played out until acceptance took root and the moment of transition arrived. Sister Clementine had begun to make her dissatisfaction known at meals. Her open complaints were hard to quell as she commented on how things were cut up, or that she wasn't given enough, or given too much. On the agitation went. One evening she looked like a light bulb and holy envy sprouted as I watched the attending sister cut her food. 'How blessed is this woman,' I pondered,' she is with her during her dying moments.' Indeed, Sister Clementine passed during the night.

The celebration of a nun's life once she has passed is one of the most dramatic events in monastic observance. For three solid days the intricate chant was devoted to her life. After the embalming her open casket was placed in the center of our choir. Lit tapers placed in six foot tall golden stands as we kept vigil day and night until her funeral. She laid there like a queen heralded the reality of life and death. Happily I obtained my favorite shift of two to three in the morning. Heading out of my cell at 1:45 the corridor greeted me like a personal escort to the choir. As my hands quietly opening the door the kneeling nun arose keeping her eyes downcast. In orchestrated fashion we genuflected together like a changing of the sacred guard. Once I got to my spot I realized it felt surreal to be kneeling there only feet from Sister Clementine. Not long after arriving I moved closer to see her, to lightly touch her hand and tell her how inspiring her life was to us all. After standing close I decided to kneel right beside her. It felt natural to be close. It was clear she was there for us, and not us for her.

Time flew as my soul dangled between the transcendent and the imminent, strung there by Sister Clementine. Not long after my replacement came.

The morning set the funeral Mass into motion leading directly to her interment in our personal cemetery. The procession was the only other time we sang Easter songs in full harmony. Sister Clementine's death opened a deep chasm of gratitude within me that I would get to walk with these women for many years to come until my time to pass would come as well. I too would have candles marking the consecration of being Carmelite as I moved into Love without end. Easter hymns would accompany my burial where all our ashes would mingle in the sacred land of prayer.

While the liturgical calendar formed the way time was marked so did the laundry. Each Sunday we would receive our new cloth napkin under our silverware. Sister Teresita who headed the laundry was brilliant. The napkins would always be stain- free, crisp, clean and bright white. The ritual of receiving a fresh one each Sunday begged efforts to keep it clean as long as possible. The arrival of a new napkin became a game where I tried to keep it crisp and white all week. This is when I realized how much of a slob I was. 'Am I really this messy? I don't remember my shirts getting dirty when I ate out in the world!' I mused. Bringing it up at recreation I learned that everyone felt the same way, how were we so messy? How did we miss our mouths so much? Or maybe the pristine cloths just revealed the human condition was one of messiness.

CHAPTER THREE

New Ways of Being

Sweet mystery unveil yourself within me...
Pulse the universe
What else is there on these roads we call paths?

IT WAS AUTUMN AGAIN. The morning found me peeling carrots in the kitchen while Sister Elijah began to churn cream for our next batch of butter. The novice mistress came in motioning me to the cooler room, 'Do you want to talk with your sister? She is on the phone!' Tears streamed down my face as I ran to the closet that housed the rotary phone. Sitting in the dark I listened to her voice wanting to capture it into a bottle so I would have it with me. 'How are you doing with the divorce...?' She trailed into a few tears. 'Not good at all,' my own voice felt so flat, stumbling into sparse words. It was overwhelming to try to talk after holding it inside for so long. This was one of the only times I was given permission talk to my sister. We rambled for a while, sharing thoughts and feelings until a light knock on the door told me it was time to go. 'Good-bye Kelly, I love you,' my lips reluctantly ended. 'Bye Kim, I love you too,' Kelly responded. I was hungry to see her.

Prayers for my family redoubled, especially for my little brother. Not only am I a sister but Kelly and I are also godmothers. Many hours of prayer were devoted to him. I begged God to let Adam feel supported with grace. I poured copious prayer for him to know how much he was held and loved by God... He was only five or six years old during the divorce. I thought seriously about leaving North Dakota for him, not that he needed me, but having family there for you is always an undeniable form of support.

Great consolation came in thinking we would all be reunited in deeper ways in heaven. It was only a passing trial and this notion gave me peace.

The year was only 1993 and so much had happened in only two years. Advent came and went, Christmas came and went, Lent came and went, Easter came and went, and every feast in between. Somewhere during that time I received a copy of the annulment. For me it was a sad piece of paper making a formal judgment on my parent's marriage not being a Sacrament. Before this had happened I wrote a personal letter to the judge. I had no idea if it would be received and was not trying to influence anything. But I needed to speak my own truth. Through example after example I told of the grace-filled moments we shared as family. I wrote of how we prayed together, how my parents taught us about love, how we made decisions to help others together. One year, I mentioned, we even gave up our family vacation to help a family in need. And another time we took care of a little girl who had lost her parents in a fire. The list sparked my own memory of all the great qualities of my family. I told the church they were wrong. 'What was all of that if it was not a Sacrament? Even if my parents are not meant to be together anymore it doesn't mean our family life was not a Sacrament,' the letter ended.

Handing me the annulment paper Mother Anna said to me, 'See Sister Annunciata, you should have peace and not be sad anymore because you now see that the marriage was not meant to be.'

'Mother Anna even when Jesus and Mary saw the crucifixion was meant to be it did not mean they did not have sadness. Sadness is normal for me to feel right now,' and I walked out of her office. Reality is what reality is. And in the face of loss, emotions are healthy to have and express.

Another big change happened this year. Our community elections took place. As a novice I did not vote but eagerly awaited the outcome. About half way through my shift in the kitchen many of the professed sisters pushed the door open, heralding our new prioress. It was my novice mistress! Excitedly they just about formed an entrance line through which she walked. I was so happy for her. She could now navigate being a leader on her own terms. It was another loss too. We had all just bonded in the novitiate and were having such an easy time. Her replacement as novice mistress was our prioress, Mother Maria Teresa. 'Whoa,' I wondered, 'how will things be, she is so strict.' The first day with us was the day my love for her tripled. Mother Maria Teresa looked like someone had taken a fifty pound weight off her shoulders, 'I love being in the novitiate,' she expressly told us up front, 'it is so much more my style.' My happiness for her grew daily as she unwound from all the responsibility of being prioress for six years.

She was quite a bit different. In some ways she was easier going and in some ways she was more demanding. For instance, she would randomly decide on recreations being quizzes for the reading at table. She was sharp as a tack and we failed to remember most everything asked. It was a nudge to not only be attentive at table, but to use our minds to actually remember what we were hearing. With all the stimulation of dishing and serving I realized that retaining the reading was much more difficult than it seemed to be. My first attempt was to take notes at table which meant foregoing eating. In the end I decided to put my best foot forward by cultivating attentiveness. Up until this point I had not realized how distracted meals were for me.

On the lighter side Mother Maria Teresa focused much less on our general mistakes. We were rarely corrected whereas our former novice mistress undertook this as one of her primary roles with us. All in all the change was not difficult as I thought it would be.

During one recreation I learned Sister Teresita was in charge of shaking out the mops I would see clustered downstairs. They gathered there through the week until she had time. Her list of duties was very long. The first time they caught my eye I was downstairs getting exercise on a mini trampoline after Compline. The wheels in my head turned, 'I could shake them all out when she was not around and put them back the same way. She would never know who did it. But her load could be lightened.' At first I looked around each week, nervous she would find out my hidden gift to her. After time her schedule became clear to me and the shaking out of the mops become part of my normal routine. In about two years this exchange would feed another story of our friendship…

Two of the greatest fruits of continual silence were the inevitable quieting of the mind and the ability to laugh at ourselves. Each nun had their own image or way they worked with personal distraction. I loved the image of Sister Rita. She would picture each thought like a little elf jumping and hopping behind her through the day. Everywhere she went, so did they. Occasionally one or two would disappear for a while, then maybe return or even be replaced by a new elf. She allowed them to do their own thing not trying to get rid of them or engage them. Over time they went their own way or would demand less of her attention. Eventually she noticed they rarely followed her at all. What a solid method to loosen the hold the mind and the pattern of thoughts it could wield.

In the silence unexpected realizations surfaced like a gift of Spirit. One evening it occurred to me that all my love and charity was impure; no matter how giving I might choose to be my motives were inevitably mixed. The realization had come out of nowhere and paralyzed me. 'Was I doing the world a disservice in my charity? Maybe I was doing more harm than good.' After weeks of confusion the moment of change came. One evening when someone needed a stool to sit upon and I ran to get them one. As I reached for it a difficult thought stopped me, 'What you are doing is really more impure than pure.' My hand stopped unable to move. The last thing I wanted to do was cause any harm but this sister was in need and my action did truly help her. In that moment a breakthrough happened, 'Just DO IT!' In that moment self-consciousness left. Just *love*. The rest is in God's hands. Relieved of the self concern over motive I was free once again to act. From here forward the action contained the realization, adding simplicity to all I might have called charity. And once again silence proved to be a school of wisdom.

As Easter moved us from spring to summer, amidst flowers and fruits and vegetables adding color to our land and our plates, my family visit arrived. It was my two year anniversary of vows and the first year my dad would visit alone. My mom was unable to visit this first year but become a close part of Carmelite life in years to come. As the day approached my own stress increased. I longed to see him but wanted more time. The thought of having to cut things short for prayer that would still be there after the visit was grueling. Confiding in the novice mistress she encouraged me to trust and accept our rules.

A surprising dramatic intervention took place. Days before the visit we were receiving a traveling painting of Our Lady of Guadalupe. The image was purported to be a channel of miracles. The requests spanned the Catholic community across the entire country. A benefactor got us onto the schedule and we were going to have her with us for four whole days!

The day she arrived I was scrubbing the long corridor perpendicular to the speak room door through which she would be brought. Sisters clambered around the image as she came through the door but I was unaware of her arrival. Scrubbing our concrete painted floor was quite a weekly chore. Fortunately the floor was masqueraded by white paint shaped like flag stone and brown borders imitating grout which hid dirt. Out of the blue Sr. Perpetua rushed down the long corridor towards me. The speed with which she made her way to me told me the painting had arrived! Her joy-filled eyes reached out to me like fingers and I dropped my dirty rag into the barely sudsy water. Grabbing my arm we rushed like little kids down the hall stopping just before turning the corner. The air was thick with Mary's presence and the fragrance of roses. Sister Perpetua and I stood facing each other holding hands. Her anticipating gaze created a moment between us engraved upon my memory, 'Sister Annunciata,' her face spoke with closed lips, 'She is so beautiful, get ready! I can't wait for you to see her!' then, she let me go.

'Haaaaaaaah' my breath drew in as I rounded the corner meeting her only ten feet away. The larger than life painting straddled the corridor as all the nuns faded into the background of my vision. They were lightly present like ambassadors standing to either side, only SHE was clear.

'You are here,' my body moved to her in clear recognition and relief. My body was magnetized towards her stopping only when it rested lightly against her image. Without any reservation I kissed her straight on the lips. In that kiss all my worry over my Dad's visit going well disappeared. The canvas of my mind, my emotions, and my psyche was washed clear in her embrace.

It will come as no surprise that the visit *was* magic. Dad entered the speak room with a solemnity in his demeanor and a simple undone love in his eyes. So much had happened for us this year.

Every moment felt like days and visit times stretched themselves through prayer. Yes, my obligation to prayer times was suspended without my asking. The very last day we planned a surprise birthday party for him since July 5th was just around the corner. Homemade gifts were created out of novitiate scrap paper, inspirational quotes and recycled wrapping paper. Like fairies joyous songs poured from our hearts to our lips. The last day another sister came in with the cake we had made as we climaxed 'Happy birthday day to you......' As the end of the song came 'Happy birthday dear Day-yad,' rose petals gathered and hid in my apron were cast upon him, 'Happy birthday to you!'

Complete. We were complete. He left and I swam like a fish deep into the waters of silence and chant, renewed from the visit and picking up my place in our community of prayer. We nuns were like lit candles holding steady vigil for all we loved and the entire world.

Most of what we ate came from what we grew. Countless were the fruits and vegetables we planted, harvested, stored, canned, froze and even pickled. Five different types of apples grew on our property yielding such abundance that apples were our normal evening fruit. We ate them whole, sauced, sliced and cooked sometimes alone with cinnamon and sometimes laden with fresh apricots, cherries, prunes or pineapple, not to mention pies and crisps. Creativity was limited only by our own imagination.

One of our special treats was asparagus on feast days. When the menu with asparagus on it came in at ten am, I would grab my clippers and bucket to cut it *fresh* for the meal! Exiting the back door a light crispness in the air would always greet me this time of day. It would expand my nostrils carrying the early sunrise aromas of the land into my lungs. My Birkenstocks (graciously provided by my family,) would attract wet blades of grass tickling my toes and casting their light dew. 'Join the party,' they seemed to beckon. Certain times of year a mist would sit upon the land up to two feet high, making it feel like we had been transported to some Celtic island. The asparagus in the patch would greet me like party favors jutting up from the earth. Sister Rita had taught me to place the cutting blade on the side of each stalk applying pressure first to see if it was tender. If it yielded easily it was ripe for our feast.

Parsnips, carrots, potatoes, horseradish, swiss chard, turnips, apricots, pears, beets, apples, figs, cherries, raspberries, sweet potatoes, onions, three colors of tomatoes, cabbage and lettuces were just a few of our farmed rewards. Some of the cabbage would be used to make the best homemade sauerkraut ever in a large four foot high, three foot diameter wooden barrel. After pounds were shredded Sister Rita would put about two feet of raw cabbage, then layer salt, layer more cabbage, more salt, and onward until the barrel was filled. A large wooden lid was sealed on top.

Swiss chard was a common vegetable brought to recreation. We grew bushel after bushel of this green leafy delectable. The entire community would sit on small stools in a circle outside the back door with large bags of the long dirt laced leaves situated in between us. One leaf was three times the size of a hand held fan and its stalk had a red hue which bled into the veins of the leaf. We would strip stalks like cutting butter. Barely had they picked one chard when it was complete and all the while chatting away. The crunchy firm texture of the leaf and sound of the 'shshshdup' stripping was utterly delightful. In addition to this I could picture the same kind of recreation back in the day of Therese in Lisieux. Women sitting in a circle while sewing or washing or perhaps preparing vegetables just like us. It felt like a thread was extending through time bearing the Eternal One through an ancient sacred lineage of women.

Food became the very way of freedom. It became the means and the end of abiding presence. Fingers squeezing beets out of their boiled husks; potatoes mashed while fresh milk and homemade butter were generously added; coring apples and filling them with our own sweet concoction of dates and brown sugar; kneading our daily bread while the leaven filling the kitchen would swell like a hot air balloon. We were bone skinny yet strong and healthy as oxen.

Food was an opportunity to grow as well. One time my ego almost won the day; I was surprised to observe its vehement protest to seeking help in a time of need. Every nun had food and flower gardens in her care. One of mine became the raspberry patch. Summers produced buckets of luscious, rose colored raspberries and we were not at a loss of ways to dress them up. Even a bowl and spoon were sufficient to please the palette. They went into cobblers, preserves, atop bread pudding, custard, or ice cream, in compote or with homemade whipped cream fresh from our cows. Actually the cream did not come to us whipped from our friendly milk providers. But it did not take long for us to pull out the hand cranked blender add a little sugar and vanilla and produce thick waves of white decadence. My sister Kelly had bought us a mixer with the handle on the top, perfect for the rising peaks that would reach the top of the metal bowl.

This patch was my first ongoing farming duty. One of the tasks was to till the three healthy berry rows. Each row stretched twenty feet long with about three feet in between them and ended abruptly at the fifteen foot deep compost pit. Tilling is generally not that hard. The machines come in a range of sizes with easy speed and direction control. Our tiller how- ever was an intimidating piece of equipment. It weighed a good ton and could easily fitting three sets of hands on its directional bar. Hesitation arose within me as Sister Rita pulled it out for first lesson. 'You have to let it run forward and keep pace with it,' she guided. 'So,' I gulped, 'it is self-propelled.'

We took it for a trial run and I could feel its power juxtaposed to my own hundred pound body. It felt like a monster that could eat me alive. The sister teaching me was smaller framed and older by 15 years yet her finesse made her a gentle master of the machine. I watched her every move figuring if I could imitate her all would go well. When it came to the North Dakota land, our animals, and our produce she was a master. Even when new calves came to visit us during recreation (our cows stayed close to our caretaker outside the cloister,) this woman corralled them with a subtle move of her wrist and her apron.

The lesson was over, too soon. Tomorrow would be my launch date.

And tomorrow came quickly. I wheeled the tiller from the shed and braced myself for the challenge. The lowest motion set me into a quick trot which made the hair on my neck rise. About half way there the partner run became exhilarating. We moved in unison across the open field and my sandaled feet sank into smooth rhythm.

The raspberry patch was only ten feet away so I prepared gripping the directional bar. I am not sure how this helped but it felt like I was readying the machine to till. As soon as we hit dirt I lowered the blade into the soil. The machine jolted and me with it as the heavy wheel blades descended about four inches. A sense of empowerment ensued, I felt like a real farmer…until halfway through the first row when my eyes caught the end point. 'Oh my,' my gut tightened. 'I am going to have to turn the corner and avoid the compost patch.'

'Sr. Rita would have given me special instructions if she thought it was going to be hard,' my thoughts consoled me. Intense concentration set in though it did little to help as the turn arrived. 'Here we go,' I turned smoothly while lurching around the corner, until….until…until what? I have no idea what happened but whatever I did caused the tiller to turn *towards* the compost instead of away, the direction I was steering. My body followed like a rag fluttering in the wind tied to the bar in a rock solid fearful grip.

Sheer desperation propelled my body to use its weight in an attempt to dig into the ground and force the tiller to shift right. The good news was the tiller yielded and avoided the full long plunge. The bad news was the tiller lodged itself into the edge of the pit dangling with its nose in the sidewall.

It was firmly lodged with no teetering to forewarn an impending drop, but I had no idea how to move it to safe ground. Sister Rita was not far away and had told me to get her if I needed help. Like a jack in the box my ego popped up. Running for her help felt so humiliating! Then reality came to me, 'Here is a true chance to walk my path by doing the right thing.' I did not walk, I ran to find her. Joy was the steam in my legs from the small breakthrough.

Her gaze was a pool of compassion evoking tears of acceptance from me. We raced to the tiller and I watched her twinkling eyes observe the crazy way it was lodged into the side. With two of us the task was easy and moments later the machine sat on firm ground.

Silence continued to have its lessons. One day during table recreation for the feast of Mary Magdalen de Pazzi we were all recalling her life. 'Remember how she was so filled with God's presence when she was cooking?' Sister Mary John mentioned. 'And she was lost in the experience for hours standing like a statue and holding the pan in which she was cooking eggs?!' Sister Perpetua added in admiringly. 'And what about when she was inflamed with the love of God and she rang the chapel bell running through the halls enjoining her sisters to love God?!' another sister added in. 'Wow I want to be like her with no inhibitions about acting on God's love alone,' I thought.

Mother Maria Teresa chimed in, 'some of the things saints do are meant to be admired, not imitated,' sharing her own thoughts around phenomena. I felt differently but her words touched in me, hitting a chord. The chord was a lingering desire for the approval of my superiors. Not long after the feast day during our hour of silent meditation a notable consolation came to me. It let me face this desire for approval. Holding a picture of Jesus crucified the tenderness of his expression caught me. The picture was from his pierced side up to the top of his head. Suddenly the picture became a live encounter between me and Jesus. A fire coursed through my veins and his side became a magnet beckoning my lips to approach. Love arose within me in force. I longed to kiss his side as he was pouring love towards me so strongly my body felt hot. As I moved towards the side the essence of Mother Maria came to me. I could feel myself carrying a feeling of her disapproval for me to get lost in the side of Jesus. This was only my own feeling; it had nothing to do with her.

The miracle of the encounter with Jesus was the freedom to choose what my heart desired. I chose the kiss, and when I did the image and the feeling completely dissolved.

CHAPTER FOUR

Sacred Solemnity

Un...
> *done...*
by YOU, oh Spirit

You spun me upon the ground of being
> *Whirled me about in realms unseen*

All the heavy pieces fell away effortlessly...

You move me by moving, O Sweet One
You love all the fear out of me
You bear the happiness I claim as my own

TIME CONTINUED TO PASS like a single breath bringing me to six months before my solemn vows in January of 1995. My prioress and I had already discussed the ceremony and I had said yes to this final step. Sister Gemma our former novice mistress was not only leader of our community, but she had also been traveling to Texas to help the founding community there. She was, in fact, the acting prioress of both leaders. These nuns left North Dakota some time in 1989. The transition had been challenging so our community was supporting like a mother hen. Up to this point there was very little I knew about the foundation, the name for a new community in a new place. They had set out before my entrance and only occasionally were their letters shared at our table recreations for feast days. I can always remember the letters of Sister Emma. She was an older nun who had worked a lifetime in the laundry and kitchen. Her letters would recollect the recollecting moments of sweeping the floor and other simple anecdotes. *This* is someone I hope to meet some day. She had a penetrating simple wisdom void of affectivity. The leader of the Texas monastery visited us once but her stay was shrouded in mystery. Not long after this leader joined one of our other monasteries. Now Sister Gemma would fly south and stay for long periods of time. She seemed to be there more than she was here.

Simple vows unfolded into deep bonds with the life. The Carmelite dream continued its magic and the time for solemn vows arrived. I was like a fish swimming in my home waters. The permanent vows ceremony was rich in solemn chant. It was a stark contrast to the bridal tones and light joyous rhythm of simple vows ceremony. The difference could be likened to a newlywed versus an older wise woman. The date stayed the same, July 16 Feast Day of Our Lady of Mount Carmel. All was in place but as the mystery of Source would have it things were spiced up unexpectedly.

I was in the chapel for my personal holy hour when it all happened. 'BUZZZZZZ, BUZZZZZZ, BUZZZZZZ, buzz, buzz,' reverberated through the halls as I rose to leave. Reaching the prioress' door the air seemed to shift and time felt like it stopped. Inside my soul was a blank white canvas. I knocked, 'Come in,' she said assuredly. Crossing the threshold my gaze fell like a beacon upon a large painting of our Lady of Grace sitting against a wall. The presence of Mary sweetly filled the room. The prioress' brow was fretted, 'the community in Texas is in need of sisters to join them. Will you go after your solemn vows?' Like a whisper I heard Mary's voice, 'They are a special community to me. I want you to go. I promise I will carry you.'

The yes was very simple, there was nothing really to consider if Mary was asking me to go. But I did not confide this whisper to my prioress so she said to think about it and let her know. One day my novice mistress asked me if I had thought about it, 'Do you want to go?' sadness in her voice. We had grown close and she had a protective nature of those she loved. 'Of course; Yes, I want to go,' the words ebbed out of my mouth both happy and sad. 'They need help so of course I will go to help.'

The next six months were a flurry of preparations for my vows and for the big move. The nuns were directed to try to pour all their skills into me; I was plunged into the office again, into the sacristy, and into the sewing room, trying to learn skills in crash course fashion.

Mother Maria Teresa, the other novices and I concentrated on having fun as much as possible. Forever will I remember running with my novice mistress out the back door with her camera bouncing around her neck. Twenty Canadian geese were standing only feet away from our back door! This woman had such a gift for hearing, appreciating and seeing beauty I could only imagine what her pictures were like. She took it upon herself to teach us how to hear birds during recreation. We had been commenting on her ability to hear and imitate them. We would listen and she would point in the direction of origin one sang or whistled. Sometimes she would whistle after them so we could learn to distinguish sounds. Honestly I felt like Helen Keller unable to get my ear to hear on its own. Suddenly one day it just happened! I started hearing birds, all sorts of birds. It was an entire world of sound. From that day forward birds were part of my world too.

In the excitement of taking solemn vows I did not reflect on how big a transition this jump to Texas would be. The move would be from a large self-sufficient group of women of all ages, women with whom into a small group of unknown women living in a converted house where I was younger by 20-30 years. This would be an adjustment that would hit me once I was there.

One of the jobs offered me for my silent retreat before vows was to prune a row of lilac trees. These fragrant beauties lined one side of the raspberry patch. Each tree stood about fifteen feet tall. I was to cut off every branch and then bring the trunk down to about three feet. The branches of blooms had just gone to seed so now was the perfect time for the dramatic hair cut. Our lilac trees were hearty; they enjoyed the overflow of manure given to the raspberry patch sitting just beside them. It was an all consuming task, perfect for a silent retreat with long hours for work. One tree's branches and trunk would make a pile large enough for three oversize trips to the burning pile on the other side of our property. All was done by hand. The limbs could be pulled if I placed a larger splayed branch like carpet on the bottom. On top of this would be clumped as many branches that would balance. Inevitably I always tried to pull too many and branches would fall off. The pulling was heavy and slow employing all the muscles in my body.

The third day I found myself dripping with sweat and feeling light-headed but continued at the same pace. The day felt unusually hot like a glove had clamped down upon the land holding the heat close to the surface. In the afternoon the property, usually dotted with sisters in their gardens, was completely empty! 'This is odd,' I thought, but continued on with my task dismissing the thought.

Not surprising the blackboard outside the chapel had a scrawled message, 'Stay inside! 110 degrees with high humidity today!' Exempt from all prayer I only saw it once the sun had set. So funny!

The entire retreat had a quality of ease. This was my home. The way the sun cast its rays into my room during the spiritual reading felt reassuring. The feeling of confidence in spending the day alone while everyone else held the normal schedule reminded me how much I belonged. There was a sense of personal ownership.

Solemn vows have an entirely different preparation. The divesting had already happened; there was no wedding gown, no white shoes and no hair to curl. In fact my hair was about as long as a military buzz. The best haircut came the day after my simple vows from my novice mistress. After that I was on my own to trim the sprouts without a mirror.

For solemn vows the preparation involved memorizing the chant responses.

To my delight Father Bernard was flown out again. My mom and dad sat in the same spot, this time divorced. I did not take for granted the great gift given to me as they sat side by side in the small seat. Even my mom's new partner attended. This would be a first meeting between the two of us and unknown at the time he and my mom would become frequent companions over the years to come. My sister and brother and my sister's family all came. The ceremony had a whirling movement of chanted call (by the sisters) and chanted response (by me in the sanctuary.) Awkwardness gave way to confidence as Father Bernard and I played and winked our way through the ritual. Once the final vows were taken he invited me up to the altar. This was only the second time I had been behind the altar. Placed upon the decorative cloth was a large book for me to enter my name officially. It was incredible we were allowed to participate in our vows so directly. My name flowed onto the page and the pen was plopped with a huge smile into Father Bernard's hand.

Kelly and I met heart to heart after the ritual. Here we were growing up. Our childhood had evolved into womanhood and each of us stepped into motherhood in our own way. What a mysterious journey we have with those close to us. At times we have heightened experiences where all the elements come together like this ceremony. Where joy and appreciation pervade the words and hugs, and where tears abound because our lives all touched in some hidden way. The blessings are impossible to count when we learn to live our lives fully. The quality of each moment interpenetrates the archetypal influence we both give and receive. We become living gateways forming a passage for our fellow sojourners into the sweetness of their own soul.

Only two weeks remained between me and the departure for Texas, nuanced by the tide of honeymoon bliss. I stayed in the novitiate for ease sake. It was nice to have a time of closure in this room that had been my own for four and a half years. My eyes drank in the final moments. I enjoyed the final days using the wobbly metal nursing table that held the many days and nights of reading writing, ruminating and exulting. I relished the small four shelves that had held my two skinny notebooks and few belongings. My corn shuck mattress received a fluffing which was about all this room would need. It was ready for the next sister.

Three distinct emotions played within me during the last two weeks. The first was a state of wistful reflection of the past four and a half years. The second was an excitement of lunging into the new adventure of Texas; and the last and most captivating was the bliss coming from my vows, which led to not caring where I was or what was coming next. We never really know how capable we are of holding immense emotions in the cavity of our heart. The more our hearts break open with love, the more all creation finds a home.

It was in this sense of timeless peace and flurry that my feet carried me out the door of the monastery July 27th, the Feast of Titus Brandsma. On the day Sister Gemma and I entered the refectory for the last time. She had flown in from Texas for my ceremony so we could return together. In the refectory all my sisters stood there as they would have stood in procession but this time facing inward and looking at us. Rare were the times we would look directly into each others' eyes making this moment incredibly tender.

Tides of emotion swirled into a whirlpool wherein my feet navigated from sister to sister for our last embrace. 'I will never see them again,' my heart ached and their eyes spoke the same. Some were crying. My dear Sister Teresita grabbed me into a full embrace and a piece of my heart thought, 'maybe she will just hold on and not let me go.' It all happened too fast. Time. Time. Why wasn't there more time? Sister Elijah and I locked our gaze, every day we had grown our friendship as we cooked for our sisters. We were perhaps closer than anyone else and now we would not grow old together as kitchen renegades. There were no words but her pure confidence cloaked in gentleness bade me a farewell as though she were waving a flag to herald me onto a glorious ship. Sister Rita gave me a gift of two homemade hearts. Mother Anna looked at me with personal pride; there was this sense in her nod of sending me off like a warrior. She had given me her words of wisdom and prophecy not only etched upon my heart, but also saved in my small notebook. Many a day we would lose ourselves in talk about God and the rigors of schedule dissolved as I showed up late to my classes. There was always something exciting about being late with the very one who enforced the strict schedule. Sister Perpetua's cheeks were bright red again as she held back tears. How many times we rolled with laughter at the jokes only the two of us seemed to 'get.' Sister Ruth kept reverting to a downward gaze with a shy reverent silence. She knew we knew each other. We shared Mary, we lived in Mary and there she would meet me and I would meet her. They were all so real, all these women and I felt so unreal. I wished to capture more of the moment, wanted to bring more love and more awareness and somehow break through to the side that rests in that which is unchanging.

After the rounds of goodbyes, we left. Our feet carried us to the door of the cloister and then through the door of the monastery. It was a door I had only walked out of once for a doctor's visit. This short perfunctory appointment fades compared to the memory of walking up to that door four and a half years earlier intending never to leave. Those initial steps as Kim Braun, steps taken in the dead of winter marked one of the biggest changes in my life. And these steps now as Sister Mary Annunciata of Jesus felt equally impactful even though the move was only to another monastery living the same lifestyle. The morning sun lay before us like a red carpet ushering us into a new era and steps emerging from my soul eagerly abounded.

How often in our lives steps, physical steps, accompany a dramatic change. It is a clue to our participation in a larger mystery. I stopped and turned; my eyes swept through the monastery drinking in the flagstone walls and simple bell tower. It was the last time I ever saw the North Dakota home of my wedding to God. And the sisters here soon became icons and symbols, leading to memories of sweetness, opening doors of inspiration. They remain my teachers today.

They came with me to San Angelo, in spirit, where a new story of the ancient unfolding was soon to begin.

ABOUT THE AUTHOR

KIMBERLY'S CONTEMPLATIVE LEANINGS BEGAN around the age of five with over ten years spent as a Carmelite nun living in a monastery. Her Masters in theology was completed in 2001 and is concentrated upon the adult spiritual journey. She enjoys officiating ritual, offering playful inspiring keynotes, writing articles and books and leading retreats. Her mission is to inspire others to live from their own YES found within. Her TEDx talk gives a taste of what it means to live a YES and is the inspiration for books two and three in her trilogy of insights. She is meditation faculty at Omega Institute and is a fellow seeker and friend on the path to living freely. Check out her CDs, videos, articles and more: www.kimberlybraun.com, www.EssenceMeditation.net.